Casting Light
on the Dark Web

Casting Light
on the Dark Web

A Guide for Safe Exploration

Matthew Beckstrom
Brady Lund

ROWMAN & LITTLEFIELD
Lanham • Boulder • New York • London

The Tor Project: CC BY 3.0-SA US
https://www.torproject.org/

The Invisible Internet Project: CC BY 3.0-SA US
https://geti2p.net/

The Freenet Project: CC BY 3.0-SA US
https://freenetproject.org/

Published by Rowman & Littlefield
An imprint of The Rowman & Littlefield Publishing Group, Inc.
4501 Forbes Boulevard, Suite 200, Lanham, Maryland 20706
www.rowman.com

6 Tinworth Street, London, SE11 5AL, United Kingdom

Casting Light on the Dark Web: A Guide for Safe Exploration is part of the Rowman & Littlefield LITA Guides series. For more information, see https://rowman.com/Action/SERIES/LITA.

British Library Cataloguing in Publication Information Available

Library of Congress Cataloging-in-Publication Data

Names: Beckstrom, Matthew, author. | Lund, Brady, 1994– author.
Title: Casting light on the dark web : a guide for safe exploration / Matthew Beckstrom, Brady Lund.
Description: Lanham, Maryland : Rowman & Littlefield, [2019] | Series: LITA guides | Includes bibliographical references and index. |
Identifiers: LCCN 2019010236 (print) | LCCN 2019012440 (ebook) | ISBN 9781538120941 (Electronic) | ISBN 9781538120934 (cloth)
Subjects: LCSH: Invisible web—Safety measures. | Dark Web—Safety measures. | Internet searching. | Privacy, Right of.
Classification: LCC ZA4237 (ebook) | LCC ZA4237 .B43 2019 (print) | DDC 025.0425—dc23
LC record available at https://lccn.loc.gov/2019010236

To my wife and son for continuing to support me through all my crazy ideas. Without them, I would not be who or where I am today.

—Matthew Beckstrom

To my parents and grandparents.

—Brady Lund

This book is dedicated to all the whistleblowers who risk everything to expose the wrongs in the world, and to the political dissidents who need avenues for communication to let the world know what is happening in places we cannot see, and to the journalists who fight to tell the stories that not everyone wants to read. This is also for everyone who wants to share, explore, and enjoy our world freely.

"Arguing that you don't care about the right to privacy because you have nothing to hide is no different than saying you don't care about free speech because you have nothing to say."

Edward Snowden, Reddit "Ask Me Anything" Session, May 21, 2015

—Matthew Beckstrom and Brady Lund

Contents

Acknowledgments

Matthew Beckstrom

I also need to say thank you to all the colleagues, mentors, and friends I have in my life who have encouraged me to ask questions, seek answers, and find ways to make a difference and a mark on the world in a positive way.

I need to acknowledge the hard work of every educator, librarian, and anyone who work hard to keep information free and open.

Finally, to Brady Lund, my co-author and friend, who took this journey with me.

Brady Lund

Major thanks to John Stewart, Kathie Buckman, Dr. Mirah Dow, Dr. Bob Grover, and Dean Wooseob Jeong for their tremendous support during my education and previous writing endeavors. To the amazing Emily Sanders-Jones, who does a lot of little things to make my life less monotonous. And, of course, to Matt Beckstrom, who has been a great colleague and mentor.

To the wonderful Emporia State University School of Library and Information Management and the many women and men who have worked to make it thrive. This book is the kind of awesome work you get to do at a great school like SLIM.

In this beautiful and diverse world, don't forget what really makes us great: empathy, communication, curiosity, and good music.

Preface

In a world of ambiguity, we often desire to have things described in terms of black and white. If you are looking for such a book on the dark web, we must apologize. There is no way to paint the dark web as a truly evil construct (as popular culture often does) or as a perfect bastion of freedom (though we might like it to be considered that way). We instead wrote this book with the aim to tell the truth and to tell it in a way that any reader can understand. It is more important to us, as the authors, to help promote informed, democratic discussion than to convince you to side with our personal beliefs. If you come out of reading this book with greater knowledge and appreciation but still believe the dark web is an evil utility, our job is well done. If you come out of reading this book with greater knowledge, appreciation, and support for the dark web, then all the better.

You will notice that this book spends relatively little time talking about the people who use the dark web—whistleblowers and the like. This is not a book to sing their praises—or to admonish them. We mention them enough to provide context, to understand who might use the dark web, but we are not so much concerned with convincing you Edward Snowden was right in what he did as with understanding why he did what he did and how he did it. Both of the authors of this book are trained as librarians, and the goal of librarians is to provide you with information—veracious facts—not to tell you how to use it. That's up to you and you alone.

We will not hide the fact that illegal activities occur on the dark web. In fact, let us state here with clarity and authority that illegal activities absolutely occur on the dark web. However, that is only one side of the story. It's the side of the story that draws clicks and brings in ad revenue, so undoubtedly it is the side you have heard far more about. But the dark web was not designed by terrorists or to be used for nefarious purposes. It was developed by the United States government to protect important communications from enemies. It was never intended for illegal uses. It was, in fact, intended for positive uses. That might sound like the good old Second Amendment debate in the US, but the arguments in this case are actually far clearer. We all know from our experience using the Internet that our privacy is not always held to the utmost standard.

We guarantee that you all have had the same experience that first got the two of us interested in researching the dark web: In Spring 2017, I (Brady) was looking to purchase a car from one of the popular used car dealers. After scrolling through the dealer's website for thirty minutes, I closed this tab and opened a new one to visit my favorite news site. I was surprised to find, about a third of the way down the page, an ad for the exact cars I was looking at earlier from the same dealer whose site I was on (plus two other dealers!). I never consented to letting my browsing behavior be tracked from site to site. I definitely did not consent to them also sending an email to the account I was logged into during my browsing. Some might call this convenience (at least your ads are relevant)—I consider it an invasion and, at the very least, creepy for the implications this data collection could one day have. So I began to seek ways in which to avoid this kind of tracking—finding a potential answer in the dark web, that "insidious technology" that I had previously only heard berated in popular culture. I was surprised, in reading more about it, what this technology was designed for and what it could offer in the way of privacy, not just in my case with the ads, but also for individuals around the world facing censorship (either of the Internet or of thought). This is the side of the dark web we want you to hear about.

I met Matt shortly after the 2017 American Library Association Annual Conference in Chicago, where I did a short presentation on the dark web and the need to research it further as a privacy technology. Matt brings the information systems background to pair with my social science background. He brings the perspective of an information worker and a PhD student/thinker (who tries, and fails, he says, to channel the writing of James Gleick and John Budd). We both bring a level of wit and humor that, at least in my case, is probably inspired by reading too many Stephen King books and listening to Eminem and The Clash as a teenager. Together we quickly began the project that would become the book you are reading now.

We have structured the text so that the chapters both build on one another and can be read in isolation. That means you can read it front to back and it will read as a complete story, or you can use it as a reference and flip around. The book also has theoretical aspects (well, kind of—not enough to bore you) and technical aspects (how to install and use the technology), but it focuses primarily on telling you what things are in a simple, approachable manner. In our minds, there are three natural divisions in the book: chapters 1–4 describe what the dark web is, its history, how it works; chapters 5–6 provide information on how to access the dark web and an index of sites to explore (with clear demarcations between sites that we recommend and those that have questionable content); and chapters 7–9 deal with issues and opportunities with the dark web and some big picture philosophical thinking. We have tried to create clear and descriptive chapter titles, but will also discuss briefly the content of each chapter here.

With this book we assume that all of our readers know absolutely nothing about the dark web. It is okay if you do—we think you will still get a lot out of this book—but we always hate books that start just one level above where we are, so that we kind of get it, but not really. By assuming you know nothing, we hope this problem is eliminated. Chapter 1, then, is simply titled "What Is the Dark Web?" If we were going to record a twenty-minute PSA for the general public on YouTube, this is what we would say you should know about the dark web. Chapter 1 also gives you a taste of our writing style, which will hopefully get you through some of the more information-intense/technical aspects of the dark web we discuss.

Chapter 2 is not directly a history of the dark web, nor is it a history of the people who use the dark web. Like we said earlier in this preface, we could give you a hall of fame of whistleblowers who demonstrate the need for the dark web, but that detracts from the overall aim of this book. If you are interested in a book about whistleblowers, there are many great ones out there, but this is not one. This history instead focuses on how the dark web is even possible. We discuss information theory, computer science, the Internet, and dark web technology. The goal is to give you a respect for the history of all these technological developments and how we view the dark web as a step in the progression of advancement.

Chapter 3 gets into deep detail about how the dark web works. Trust us, it is worth reading, even if it is technical—and it gets easier from there. Chapter 4 is written to be conversational, like a Q&A. Here we have a list of myths about the dark web and how we would respond to them. We also mention the dark web scans that you hear about on TV and whether they actually do what they say they do.

Chapter 5 is your guide to installing the three major dark web platforms: Tor, Freenet, and I2P. Tor is the platform that is typically referred to when one talks about the dark web, but all three we discuss here have a good deal of popularity. Much of the information in the early part of this chapter is available on the sites of the individual platforms, and we encourage you to visit these sites to read more about the three platforms. The second part of the chapter discusses the similarities and differences between the platforms and addresses some questions about which platform is right for you.

Chapter 6 aims to help address a major challenge for the dark web platforms: lack of a search engine. In addition to a history of dark web sites, we provide an extensive index of these sites with information about them and guidance about whether we would recommend visiting the site to our minister. Chapter 7 dives deeper into the legal and ethical considerations with the dark web. We talk about the history of illegal activity on the dark web and distinguish between the positive and unsavory aspects of the dark web.

Chapter 8 is our attempt to further the discussion about the dark web. If our book moves you to explore the dark web further, or work to support it, chapter 8 will give you some guidance on how to do so. We appeal to the spirits of Everett Rogers and Thomas Kuhn to raise the true dark web into the public consciousness. (If you do not know who those two are, consider yourself lucky you did not have to take a semester-long course on them, but also read up on them because, hey, they are the most influential social theorists of the twentieth century.) We also discuss the untapped potential for legitimate commercial ventures on the dark web.

Chapter 9 ties everything together with the surprisingly similar stories of how the Internet was viewed in the early 1990s and the dark web is viewed today. It is a gem of the Internet Archive that we hope will leave you thinking and wanting to investigate the dark web further.

Writing *Casting Light on the Dark Web* was a passion. We hope that this book establishes a greater discussion of the dark web in the global society. It does not really matter what side of the issue you come down on; what matters is that we talk about the dark web while we have the opportunity and do not let it fall to obscurity or get completely overrun by illegal content that forever tarnishes its potential to bring benefit to the world. So give this book a read and then let someone else have a read and talk about it. Let's start a critical discourse about whether we should protect this technology, police it, or allow it fall to obscurity. Do not let time decide for us!

Important Terms Defined

Anonymous Web: Generic, neutral term to refer to services/locations on a communication network that provides enhanced anonymity. For instance, the dark web is a communication network that provides enhanced anonymity.

ARPANET: A forerunner and technical foundation of the modern Internet.

Bridge: Connections that are not publicly listed and are generally considered to be censorship resistant.

Cookies: Packets of information that identify and describe a user/website and/or their behavior. These packets of information are what allow a webpage to display ads for items you viewed earlier of a different website.

Dark Net: A special network that lies over or outside of the Internet. An analogy for the dark net is that the dark net is to the dark web as the Internet is to the World Wide Web. Dark web sites lie in the dark web, which runs on the dark net, just as .com sites lie in the World Wide Web, which runs on the Internet.

Dark Web: Describes a collective group of web pages that can only be accessed using special browsers/networks.

Deep Web: Web pages that exist on the World Wide Web but are hidden behind permissions or login pages (authentication).

Hypertext Transfer Protocol (HTTP): Set of rules/procedures for communicating data on the World Wide Web. When typing a web address, this protocol is referenced (by the inclusion in the address of http://www).

Internet: Global system of connected computer networks.

Network: A system of connections. In terms of computer science, this is generally connections between a group of computers/servers that communicate (send data/information) between one another.

Node: One computer or server participating in the dark web network.

Peer-to-Peer: Communication network where members have the ability to directly distribute to and retrieve information from one another.

Relay: Connections between the computers/servers participating in the dark web network.

Surface Web/Clear Net: What we normally call "the Internet." Web pages we interact with on a regular browser (e.g., Internet Explorer, Google Chrome) that do not require special permissions or logins to access.

Tor: The Onion Router, one specific dark web network. Sometimes, Tor is referred to interchangeably with the dark web, since it is by far the most widely used of these networks.

Virtual Private Network (VPN): Encryption that allows for direct connection to a site without interference or tracking. Disguises the location from which a user is connecting (often used to connect to content that is restricted in a certain country; e.g., video and audio streaming applications).

World Wide Web: Interlinked information resources accessed through the Internet.

1

What Is the Dark Web?

WHAT IS THE DARK WEB?

What is the dark web? We see it depicted in movies and the media as an insidious forum where criminals purchase drugs and take down governments. But how true is that? Is there really no merit to the dark web, or have facts simply been clouded by sensationalism? We believe the dark web is not quite as dark as it is made out to be. We find that, as with many things in this world, there are two very different sides to the story. It is our goal to tell the side of the story that is often neglected. In this book, we will show how the dark web is used to protect people and provide privacy. We will show you how and—more important—why the dark web was developed. We will introduce you to ways to safely access and explore the dark web from the comfort of your own home, and why you would want to. Welcome to our straight, no-bull guide to the dark web. Join us as we cast light upon its shadowy veneer.

The Deep Web

The term *dark web* does not necessarily mean a place where illegal activities occur or dark deeds are performed. The dark web is called dark for the same reason the night is called dark: you cannot see what all is there. Whereas on the mainstream Internet anyone with a computer and a web browser can visit Google and search the entirety of knowledge indexed within it, the dark web is hidden.

The dark web is part of a broader concept called the deep web. The deep web is simply defined as any portion of the Internet that is not readily accessible to the average Internet user. The deep web includes sites that are behind corporate firewalls or are behind authentication or pay-walls that are available only to subscribers or to a limited number of individuals. Have you watched a Netflix video online recently? Read a paid article on NYTimes.com? Maybe you have paid some bills or purchased something on Amazon? Surely you have logged into email or Facebook? All of these are examples of deep web content. You cannot just go online and freely access this content. You had to log in. You had to dig beyond the surface of what is on the website to access content buried under a login screen. Hence, the term *deep web*.

The deep web is a very good thing. We do not want our hidden Facebook profiles searchable on Google. (That is why we made them hidden!) We definitely do not want our banks to list all our account numbers and financial details in a publicly available database. Netflix and the *New York Times* are not going to make enough money to support their businesses if everyone with an Internet browser can access all their content. In a capitalist society, the deep web is what makes e-commerce possible, and ideally the vast majority of sites on the Internet will be deep web sites.

Content that is considered part of the deep web is not indexed in search engines. Indexing is a process that search engines use to create lists of accessible information on pages. When a website is indexed, the words that appear on the page are put into a list of similar terms. Search engines like Google or Bing will only index and make available sites that their web crawling indexers can locate and have permission to index. Pages on the deep web are not accessible by search engines, so they cannot log in to index them. Again, we do not want our proprietary content freely available in your average Google search, so thank goodness for the deep web. It encourages the online development that has produced all the major websites we enjoy today and creates millions of jobs in e-commerce and web development.

The dark web is a part of the deep web, or a subset of it. The dark web, like the deep web, consists of sites that are not indexed by Google or other similar search engines. Unlike the traditional deep web sites previously discussed, however, dark web sites are not indexed because of system design rather than site design. Dark web sites are not necessarily buried beneath login screens. They are hidden by an invisibility cloak. Google cannot index what it cannot access but also cannot index what it cannot see.

Here is another way to think of it. The Internet can be broken down into two major divisions, the regular, visible, or surface web—stuff I can type into an address bar or Google and pull right up on my computer with no extra steps—and the deep web. It is estimated that the deep web is roughly 90 percent of all the information available on the Internet (unfortunately, it is not possible to come to a specific number since the deep web is mostly hidden or unavailable). For instance, Netflix has maybe ten publicly available pages—the home page, the account creation page, FAQs, Help, etc.—and millions of deep web pages, with information about the films, user accounts, and payment forms. Sites like Facebook are similar. They have a portion of their site that is accessible on the surface web. You can find pages, search content, or view information that users have made visible. They also have a much larger portion of their site that is not visible; it is hidden behind logins, or only visible to close friends. Take the deep web, then, and divide it into two parts: the deep web and the dark web.

Another very common way to visualize the Internet is by using the iceberg analogy. Think of an iceberg floating in the ocean. The small part, roughly 10 percent of the iceberg, is above the waterline and is visible. This is the visible or regular Internet. The remaining 90 percent under the water is the deep web. Then take the last little spike at the bottom, roughly 5 percent of the underwater portion, and that is the dark web. Once again, the actual percentage is really unknown. It is difficult to fully know how much is on the deep or dark web.

What if you do not like icebergs (or still do not understand the relationship between the deep and dark web)? Think of rectangles and squares. Quick geometry lesson: all squares are rectangles (have two equal sides) but not all rectangles are squares (have four equal sides). The deep web is like rectangles, and the dark web is like squares. The dark web is part of the deep web, because it shares the quality of not being accessible on the surface of the web, but the dark web also has qualities that differentiate it from the deep web. It is not hidden because of authorization issues. It is hidden because its creators have taken steps to make it invisible to the average user. The average deep web site has not undergone this process to make it completely invisible. It cannot be said that a deep web site is a dark web site unless it has undergone this process, just as it cannot be said that a rectangle is a square unless the sides have been squished until they are equal.

WAYS TO ACCESS THE DARK WEB

The dark web is not one single place. It is a concept that describes several online networks, just like the concept of social media describes thousands of different websites and platforms. Speaking of the dark web as though it is a single network is like speaking of social media as though Facebook, Twitter, Instagram, Snapchat, Myspace, and all the many other platforms past and present are the same thing. We know that Facebook and Twitter, though they have similar goals of facilitating communication and spreading ideas, are very different from the user's perspective. One has completely different functionalities from the other. The only thing they have in common is that underlying philosophy. Same thing with the dark web. There are all kinds of dark web networks, each of which provides different functionalities.

The most common dark web network is the Tor network (also called the Tor Project). The Tor network, previously known as the Onion Router, is a dark web network that is accessible only through a specially designed browser. The creator of Tor (which just happens to be the US government) discovered that creating the network within the shell of a Firefox browser increases security rather than having the network open in a default browser. To access Tor, then, you have to download and install this modified browser on your computer, just as you would any new browser (more on this process in chapter 5).

The I2P network, or the Invisible Internet Project, and Freenet are the two other most popular dark web networks. Let us analyze each one of these networks in greater detail.

Freenet

The Freenet network is a distributed peer-to-peer network designed to promote censorship-resistant communication and anonymous publishing. Freenet uses a distributed file storage system. When information is inserted into a Freenet site, it is broken into pieces and stored on different servers around the Internet. When a user accesses a particular piece of information, that information is retrieved from multiple sites. The system uses this distributed network to protect the anonymity of the person uploading information and the person retrieving it.

Think of a pirate burying her treasure. She does not put all the treasure in one place, because if she did and someone found it . . . well, they would have all her treasure! So, she hides it in chests scattered all across the seas. Now, if she wants to put that treasure back together to purchase a new private jet (because this is a very anachronistic pirate), she has to pull from multiple treasure chests. Distributed file storage hides your treasure all over the web so that it cannot all be stolen together and then pieces it back together when it is time to make a withdrawal (i.e., you want to view or use the content).

Freenet also uses encryption technologies in all its communications to help protect privacy. Encryption is like that invisibility cloak. The invisibility cloak bends light so you cannot see what is there. Encryption disguises online content so that, as far as an outside observer or computer can tell, the encrypted content could be the answer to the mystery of life, winning lottery jackpot numbers, a bunch of random words typed in a document, or literally nothing at all. Encryption is especially beneficial for anyone who wants to publish information that is controversial or dangerous. If someone lives in a country that blocks the majority of Internet traffic, this could be one of the only ways for them to publish information and make it available to others around the world. Am I sending political information to dissidents in North Korea or sending them a funny cat video? The North Korean government will never know (at least in theory).

I2P

The Invisible Internet Project, or I2P, works similarly to the Freenet platform. The biggest difference is that I2P is basically a network on top of the Internet. Freenet and Tor essentially create tunnels or niches within the existing Internet to house their content. This means that the Internet still exists around the networks. For instance, within the Tor browser you can still access traditional World Wide Web sites. The hidden content is like a good Easter egg in a movie. While it is there, within the normal corpus of the Internet, you are just not going to find it unless you are intentionally looking for it or manipulating it in a certain way. I2P, on the other hand, functions like the traditional Internet, but is not part of the Internet; rather, it is a completely separate network.

When your computer connects to the I2P network, it becomes a node on the network. Traffic passes through your computer from one node to other nodes, and your requests are also routed through other nodes on the I2P network. It uses a sophisticated routing system that allows each user to create their own links of routes. The longer the route, the better the security. It is like a super-secure cell phone relay. Each node your access is routed through will "ping" like a cell phone tower when you use it. The goal is to create so many pings at the same time that no outside observer can tell which cell phone tower you are actually using.

Since I2P uses its own network, it is particularly useful for someone who wants to use different kinds of Internet communication besides regular web browsing. It can be used for instant messaging, secure email, and peer-to-peer file sharing systems. Do not expect to find Facebook or CNN on I2P. Visiting this network can be like stepping into a completely different universe of the Internet.

Tor

The largest and most popular dark web application is the Tor browser. When a connection to the Tor network is created, it routes traffic through a network of nodes just as with Freenet. (Unlike Freenet, you do not automatically become a node yourself when you use Tor; you must install specific software to do it.) With each node along the chain, your traffic is re-encrypted and then routed to another node. Eventually your traffic request reaches an exit node (a final node in a chain), where it is redirected to the regular Internet or to a special .onion website. This type of routing traffic through the Internet with encryption is called onion routing. Why? Because onions have layers, of course, and so does node routing and encryption. The process adds layers to your traffic to make it private and secure. An outsider would have to dig through all these layers of your web browsing "onion" (which is nearly impossible) to see who you are and what you are accessing.

Tor was developed at the United States Naval Research Laboratory and was used to support secure communication with whistleblowers and undercover operatives across the globe for nearly a decade before being released in 2002 to the general public for use. While it is still used by governments and organizations to protect whistleblowers (one of the major reasons many governments still support the dark web, even though they paint it as evil at the same time), many new uses of Tor have emerged in the past two decades. It quickly gained popularity after being released to the public for its ease to learn and high level of anonymity, and it grew as users discovered new ways for the network to be utilized. Tor has likely now evolved to the point where it could never be completely shut down, even with coordinated efforts by several powerful governments. The "best" that can be done is to target specific websites on the network and try to expose the identity of site owners through detective work.

Other Dark Web Networks

There are many lesser known and less popular dark web networks—likely well over one hundred worldwide. Often these are simple, small connections called friend-to-friend (often denoted as F2F) networks, or peer-to-peer (often referred to as P2P) networks. A friend-to-friend network can be a simple connection between two or more computers on the Internet using an encrypted connection to share information or communicate.

Think of a friend-to-friend network like old-school tin can telephones. If I have a can and you have a can, then we can talk to each other and (theoretically) have a conversation. However, anyone who might want to come along the line and spy on our conversation will have a very difficult time doing so, since we are only connected by a string that is useless without something to translate the sound. On the other hand, if we are using a long tube to communicate (think traditional computer communication and exchange), all that somebody needs to do is cut a hole in the tube and they can hear our entire conversation. The dark web friend-to-friend network ensures that only those with cans are hearing the conversation and that no unwanted sleuths are listening in on another line.

Examples of applications that can be used to create friend-to-friend networks are Retroshare, WASTE, GNUnet, and OneSwarm. Peer-to-peer networks are created via computers linked together using specialized software that facilitates the transfer of files or transactions. They do not need to exist on the dark web, but the dark web obviously provides the privacy layer that insulates that string between our cans. Peer-to-peer applications are often used to share music, movies, pictures, and other files.

We will spend more time in chapter 3 discussing how the dark web works. That chapter will cover how the connections and networks that make up the dark web create privacy and use encryption to protect communication.

WHAT IS THE VALUE OF THE DARK WEB?

The dark web resulted from the need to protect personal information and activities on the Internet. Each of the large dark web networks—I2P, Freenet, and Tor—had its roots in the desire to ensure basic protection and anonymity for all Internet users. As will be discussed throughout the remaining chapters of this book, there are nefarious activities perpetrated on the dark web. There are, undoubtedly, people who use these networks for purposes beyond that for which they were designed. But this is true of many things in the world today. If we allow the misuse of some users to detract from the true mission of these platforms, then we are failing to recognize what can be one of the most valuable tools for freedom and privacy the world has ever seen.

Freenet was created to offer a platform of distributed communication. It is a way for people to publish information, either blog posts, email, or web pages, in a form that is anonymous. It allows publishers to create and publish information without the fear of censorship. In areas of the world where citizens are not protected by freedom of speech, or where government or militaries censor information, access like that provided by Freenet is necessary for citizens to share information. It also allows individuals to view and access materials that might otherwise be blocked or censored where they live.

I2P was created with complete anonymity and censorship resistance in mind. The idea was to create a different network on the regular Internet that did not have the same weaknesses. I2P creates a secure chain of nodes that allow users to communicate with strong encryption, and a connection that is not traceable. Since I2P is more of an interface to the Internet, it allows the user to use a larger variety of tools than Freenet or Tor allow. I2P allows instant messaging, email services, file sharing applications, and almost any other kind of Internet communication.

Tor, by far the most popular dark web network, was created to allow anonymous and protected communication on the visible web. The idea was to create a network that would encrypt the communication, and route it in a way to prevent monitoring or tracking. Tor also offers services that are available only through Tor nodes. These services on the network usually have a .onion network address instead of the common .com address. Since these services are available only on the Tor network, and typically do not interface with the visible web, they offer the user more anonymity. Having a higher level of anonymity allows people to post or access information they otherwise might not be able to where they live.

WHAT CAN THE DARK WEB DO FOR ME?

We believe that everyone can benefit from the dark web no matter their situation, but how you specifically use the dark web will vary greatly depending on your personal situation. Let us discuss a couple of possible situations.

For the average Internet user, increased security and privacy may not be of high concern. But, as high-profile leaks of user information on major websites continuously illustrate, the Internet is not a particularly secure place and online companies do not always do the best at protecting our privacy. As we browse the web, we are constantly broadcasting our activities all over the place. Personal information—what sites we visit, how long we spend on them, what we look at on certain sites, what we purchase, what kind of computer and browser we use, and where we are located—is constantly being collected and used by advertisers, governments, and corporations. Most of the time this information is being collected and used without our knowledge or permission.

You can get a glimpse of this collection in action right now on your personal computer. Open a browser and click on your connection information tab to the left of the web address (on Google Chrome it will be a small icon of a lock"; on Internet Explorer/Edge it will likely be the I icon or globe icon). There will be an option within this tab called "cookies." Cookies are pieces of information about you and your computer. They may store information such as your login credentials (so you do not have to log in again each time you revisit a site), your browsing history, how you found the site, and from where you are accessing the site. What is worse is that the code embedded in the cookie is mostly indecipherable to us, so we cannot really even tell what information a specific site is collecting. Cookies are an enigma because they can certainly improve your browsing experience, but is it worth it to expose all that personal information for a better experience?

Dark web services can prevent the collection of this information and keep the average user invisible. The dark web can crumble cookies. It can protect our information from being hijacked and used against us. There have been many examples of these types of private communications being hijacked. Social media sites, particularly, are frequent victims of data breaches and unauthorized use of personal information.

What about journalists who travel around the world writing about conflict or human rights violations? They need a way to communicate with other journalists and with their publications. The dark web gives them the ability to transmit information securely. They can send emails and chat without fear of their transactions being monitored or blocked. Residents of countries that prevent full access to the Internet, or that monitor communication on the Internet, can use that same access given by the dark web to communicate with the world outside their country. They can seek information for their personal needs that they otherwise would not have access to, or provide and publish information to people outside their country on what is happening inside their country.

Businesses, corporations, and nonprofit and government organizations such as libraries and international and politically affiliated charities can use the dark web to protect their employees and patrons from unintended monitoring or eavesdropping. They can use it to transfer confidential information in a way that helps to prevent it from being intercepted or stolen.

We will explore more ways to use the dark web in chapter 6, and show how to reap more rewards from using the dark web in chapter 8.

The dark web is a tool. As with any tool, it can be extremely useful and dangerous at the same time. Think of cars. Cars are an extremely useful item. We use them every day and as long as we use them responsibly and carefully they help us get from point A to point B. But cars can be used incorrectly and consequently do major damage. Used properly, the dark web can be an incredible facilitator for private communication and the exchange of ideas. You can communicate without the fear of some person, corporation, or government watching or collecting what you say or do. Used improperly, the dark web can be everything that the sensationalist news reports say it is. We want to make sure that the dark web is used properly and believe the way to do this is through encouraging a large population of ethical users who understand its immense benefits. The dark web exists as a modern Wild West. Now it is our time to wrangle it up and use it for the advantage of our society. Join us for the ride!

2

History of the Internet and Dark Web

It is important to make a few distinctions at the start of this chapter. The purpose of this chapter is not to provide a history of those who use the dark web, per say, but rather the history of technological innovations that made the infrastructure of the dark web possible. In other words, this is a history of dark web technology, not necessarily a history of how that technology has been used. For that reason, we start our history with information theory and the Internet.

Yes—as we state throughout this book—the Internet and the dark web are not the same, but the latter would certainly not exist without the infrastructure of the former. We believe that one cannot begin to understand how the dark web works without understanding (on a basic level) how the Internet works; and one cannot understand how the individual networks (Tor, Freenet, I2P) work without first understanding how dark web networks work in general. So we have devised a linear, chronological progression from the foundations of computer science, communication and information theory, and electrical engineering, up through the dark web networks available today. We, of course, could not fit in every detail we would have liked, but ask that you consider this an introduction, and encourage you to explore further.

BEGINNER'S OVERVIEW OF INFORMATION THEORY

We will not attempt to explain information theory and its contributions to our modern world in any great detail—because there are semester-long courses at MIT that cannot even accomplish this task. We do, however, want to touch on some of the figures that we believe are important to making computer science and information networks (like the dark web) possible. We are going to focus on three figures of the mid-1900s that we find particularly crucial to the eventual development of the Internet (and, subsequently, the dark web): Alan Turing, Vannevar Bush, and Claude Shannon. Again, there were many important figures in addition to these three, and we encourage you to research further if this brief overview of information theory intrigues you.

Alan Turing is widely considered the father of computer science, having described in the mid-1930s a computing machine—"a single machine which can be used to compute any computable sequence."[1] Such a machine would be capable of "memorizing" and "recognizing" data patterns. Turing's later design of a Boolean logic multiplier machine played a crucial role in military efforts in World War II. Though the Turing machines were not practical compared to the memory capabilities of modern computers utilizing random-access memory for data storage (his sequential memory is the meta-equivalent of cassette tape versus MP3 format for audio storage), the math Turing outlined in "On Computable Numbers, with an Application to the Entscheidungsproblem" and his dissertation, "Systems of Logic Based on Ordinals," is the theoretical foundation of the field of computer science (later used interchangeably with the name *informatics*).

Vannevar Bush is less widely recognized than the theorists listed directly before and after him, but that is not so much a critique of Bush as a statement on how important the contributions of Turing and Shannon are on information theory today. Besides being an instructor to Shannon, Bush inspired information professionals across the spectrum with his publication "As We May Think."[2] Bush's work with electronic data storage would directly influence the fields of library and information science. The Memex system that he described predicted, on an organization-wide level, the information systems with which library professionals work extensively today: the Integrated Library System (ILS).[3] These systems aim to capture large swaths of human knowledge and catalog it for convenient access. As technology improves, more electronic resources are directly linked to the catalog for access, and users have the functionality to save preferences and notes, all within their smartphones. These same ideas inspire the design of digital libraries, aggregators, and even search engines. Bush worked directly with our next figure, Claude Shannon, while Bush was an instructor and Shannon a student at Massachusetts Institute of Technology (MIT).

The study of information was radically transformed by Shannon's "Mathematical Theory of Communication," something simple yet at the same time so revolutionary that aftershocks radiated throughout the hard and social sciences (much to the chagrin of some academics). Originally published by Shannon as a series of two papers while he worked at Bell Labs (at the time, Bell was part of AT&T),[4] the theory was published in monograph form in 1949, with additional writings about the applications of the theory by Warren Weaver.[5] Shannon's original paper has been cited over 100,000 times—and for good reason. Shannon introduced a mathematical model of noise in a communication channel. Think of a big game of "telephone" and how error and misinterpretation can lead to a complete distortion of a message; the same problems are relevant with actual telephones and all other networks that involve a message being passed over a medium—from face-to-face verbal communication to Internet connections. In providing the concepts of information entropy and the bit, Shannon paved the way for virtually all communication technology that we enjoy today.

BASIC HISTORY OF THE INTERNET

The Internet itself began as a United States government project called ARPANET. ARPANET, which stands for Advanced Research Projects Agency Network, was developed and implemented by the Department of Defense. The concept of tARPANET was proposed in the early 1960s by several computer scientists to the Department of Defense to create a new type of computer network that allowed more efficient communication. The DOD agreed, and money was allocated to the design and development of the network.

One of the biggest new ideas for ARPANET was the idea of packet switching instead of circuit switching, as was traditionally used in communication at that time. Circuit switching is that way that telephone networks operated from the invention of the telephone. You pick up your phone, and by dialing a series of numbers, you are creating a circuit, or a dedicated connection between your phone and another phone. There are no other phones on this type of communication; the entire connection is dedicated to your conversation. Remember the pictures of operators sitting in a large room with cables strung everywhere as they physically made connections between phones? These operators were eventually replaced with technology that made the connections quicker, but the infrastructure required to make the connections became very expensive and burdensome. Packet switching replaced this technology.[6]

Packet switching is more effective because it can use the same physical connection for multiple simultaneous communications. It uses a series of data "packets," or small bundles of information that are sent between devices on the network. They are routed around the network using different types of "addresses." At the top of each packet is a bit of information about who is sending that packet and to whom it is being sent. Think of these packets as digital envelopes. On the outside there is a return address that says who is sending the letter, and also a recipient address that says where it is being directed. You put your envelope in the mailbox (or put your packet on the network), and it is picked up by the mailman, who takes it to a sorting facility where the address is read and it is sent to another facility. On the network, your packets are sent to various routing devices that use the recipient address to send it to another device on the network until it is finally "delivered" to the correct recipient.

With packet switching, a single telephone line that was designed to have a single conversation on it could now be used to have many conversations. In other words, it turned the individual "post office" of communication into a distribution center that could facilitate communication in many directions, across various distances, at the same time.

At the time ARPANET was developed, the infrastructure in the United States to support a packet-switched network was not in place, so the DOD was forced to create their own connections between the offices that were using ARPANET. This same undertaking of building up the information (communication) infrastructure occurred with telegraph lines during the American Civil War. Thanks to the war, and the need to quickly and efficiently communicate messages across the frontlines, the world's strongest communications infrastructure was constructed.

This initial ARPA network was not, as is often mentioned in pop culture, solely developed to protect communications of the DOD in the event of a nuclear war; however, this proved to be a substantial benefit of the network. With the packet-switching technology, a network like ARPANET would be extremely useful in a major catastrophe like a nuclear war. The communications routed on the network could be quickly re-routed in the event that a portion of the network were to become disabled. The DOD quickly realized this benefit, and ARPANET was expanded to provide this service.[7]

By the early 1970s ARPANET had expanded from its home in California to the East Coast. More and more sites were added to it, including some universities. Remember, at this point, ARPANET was not the Internet, and it was accessible only from government installations and some universities. There was no reason for the users on ARPANET to be concerned with security or privacy. They were aware of everyone who was on the network, so the information that was available was appropriate for the users. As time moved on, though, more and more nongovernmental users began to connect to ARPANET. In the mid-1980s the network was restructured to move the military nodes into their own separate network called the Defense Data Network. Now ARPANET was split into two networks: the military network and the civil network. They were still connected, but there was a gateway between them.[8]

There were many other networks similar to ARPANET by the 1980s. The ideas of packet switching and computer-based communication and collaboration had taken off, and more groups, agencies, and governments wanted to take advantage of this technology. In the late 1980s there were hundreds of separate networks all across the United States, each created to serve a specific purpose. Most were government networks created by different agencies to facilitate communication, some were educational institutions created to collaborate on projects, and some were created by independent organizations. Each one modeled the design of its network based on the earlier networks, but also fine-tuned the way it worked. Consequently, they all kind of worked similarly to each other, but a little bit better. One network in particular during this time that moved the technology forward was the National Science Foundation Network (NSFNET). It was created in 1985 to promote advanced research and education networking. It used a new type of communication protocol called TCP/IP (Transmission Control Protocol/Internet Protocol) that was more efficient in routing packets around the network. This protocol would become the primary communication protocol for the Internet.

With the explosive growth of communication networks in the United States, the idea of connecting them began to emerge. NSFNET began to create connections between the different educational and science-based networks. As the networks connected, they needed to standardize the communication protocols they used. To connect to the NSFNET, they were forced to adopt the TCP/IP protocol. The NSFNET grow so fast, they created another basic Internet technology, the "backbone." The idea of a backbone was to create a central hub that connected all the different networks. It stretched across the United States, and allowed even more sites to connect. With the network backbone in place, more and more networks connected, and more networks were created. International links were created to Canada, Mexico, and several countries in Europe.[9]

Remember, at this point, this "Internet" was still only educational, scientific, and government networks. This was not the Internet as we know it today. The only people on the network at this time were there for similar reasons. There may have been thousands or tens of thousands of people who had access to the overall network, but they basically kept to their own local networks, and occasionally sent information to users on other networks using the connections between them. There was little concern for privacy. Many of the networks that were connecting were dealing with important or secure information. They dealt with this security by keeping sensitive materials on the local networks. Once again, since the users on the networks were all working with the same goals in mind, security was not an issue of a high enough concern to deal with on the whole.

In 1990 everything changed. ARPANET was officially decommissioned, and commercial Internet service providers (ISPs) appeared. Now, for the first time, the average computer user with no educational or scientific interests could connect to the network. In 1995 NSFNET was officially decommissioned and the remaining Internet backbones were connected, creating what we consider to be the Internet today. Growth continued, with more Internet providers giving access to more average users. People quickly discovered the benefits of fast communication using email and Internet chat. Files were shared and traded. When Tim Berners-Lee created the World Wide Web and the communication standards we use in Internet browsers like Internet Explorer, Chrome, and Firefox, people were able to browse and view all types of material from all over the world. Entertainment began to grow exponentially during this time. As speeds and access increased, people began to use the Internet to learn, for entertainment, and to shop. Commercial entities quickly realized the impact the Internet was having on everyday life, and started putting a presence on the Internet. They found that Internet sales provided faster and more efficient experiences for their customers. Government agencies began to post information for the communities on the Internet.

All this growth came with problems. Some people on the Internet figured out ways to disrupt communication. Internet viruses, worms, and malware began to rise almost as quickly as the Internet grew. These disruptions forced Internet users to protect themselves. Antivirus software emerged to solve some of these issues. Networks began to protect themselves by putting firewalls between themselves and the Internet. Antivirus software and firewalls would continually inspect the traffic that was passing over the network and determine whether any of that traffic was harmful or dangerous. Most of these attacks were not personal. They were simple viruses designed to create chaos, or worms that would take down networks.

Some attacks, however, were very directed. Cybercrime became a new issue that corporations, governments, and other entities had to deal with. A darkness began to creep up from the Internet of criminals using the Internet to steal or to destroy. They would use the Internet to break into networks to steal information, or to take down companies. They would use direct attacks against competitors to prevent them from doing business. This type of cybercrime created new industries formed to stop or block these types of attacks. Eventually, governments were forced to step in to help protect not only themselves, but commerce in general.[10] The Internet had become such a vital resource for commerce and trade that it was imperative it not be interrupted. New tools were developed that allowed greater intrusion into the communication going across the Internet. People and organizations could watch, monitor, and record communications and other activities. Internet service providers, in order to maintain the integrity of their networks, began to monitor their users. They would watch for viruses or attacks and stop them if they were coming from their internal networks or trying to get into the networks.

Adoption of the Internet across the world moved at an ever-increasing pace. More and more countries jumped on the Internet, such that it truly became a global network. Of course, not everyone was happy with all the information that was available. In some countries, the ideas and beliefs of other countries were not acceptable, and the offended countries quickly moved to block them. It is hard to allow access to a resource that is as all-encompassing as the Internet, yet not allow it all. Think back to the way the Internet was designed: a network of devices connected together to share information. That is what the Internet continues to be, a really large network designed to be open. We have had to force it to be protective. We put up walls and safeguards to prevent all that openness, and it does not always work. Viruses continue to infect us. Malware continues to trick people, and entities continue to attempt to break into places they should not.

UNDERSTANDING PRIVACY
NEEDS ON THE EARLY INTERNET

On the early Internet, privacy was often a second thought. The separate networks each kept their secrets from the other networks. Authentication was the standard way of protecting resources. To access a particular resource, you needed to know the username and password. This simple security was typically ample to protect what was meant to be kept secret. Criminals were generally not interested in the early Internet, because the cost to connect to the network far outweighed any potential gains.

Once the general public was allowed on the Internet, security and privacy became increasingly needed. Websites were not designed to keep people out. They were made to allow people in. Logging was created to allow the site operators to know who was accessing their sites, and where they were from. Basic browser and operating system information was broadcast with each transaction. This was of little concern, though. Most people were not concerned with privacy or security.

Eventually, viruses and malware began to increase. There were now enough people using the Internet, and a low enough cost of connecting, to entice criminals. Unsuspecting users were easily duped into accessing malicious programs. Antivirus software was developed to help protect computers. These beginning applications, however, did not address privacy concerns. They were mostly focused on locating and blocking viruses.

Encryption was virtually nonexistent on the early Internet. There was no immediate need for secure connections, and the speeds that were available at the time made encryption a difficult technology. The Internet backbones had reliable and decent speeds, but the final connections between the ISP and the end user typically used a telephone line and a slow modem. Page load times were anywhere from thirty seconds to several minutes for pages with mostly text. Encrypting these same pages would have significantly slowed down the page load times. Nevertheless, Netscape, a company formed to create a web browser called Navigator, created Secure Sockets Layer (SSL) security for its browser in 1994. This early encryption technology worked, but it required that the server software and the browser both support SSL. This early in the adoption process, the slow side effects meant that there were not a lot of sites that supported SSL connections. Two years later, in 1996, the Internet Engineering Task Force (IETF) realized the opportunities with encryption and SSL and worked with Netscape to improve the technology; eventually, it took over the maintenance and control of SSL. The IETF is a standards organization that was created to form partnerships between interested parties on the Internet to facilitate and coordinate standards for Internet users. Once control of the SSL technology was moved to the IETF, it started to grow in adoption rates. Also, as the speeds of connections increased, and the technology that enabled secure connections became more available, more sites adopted the technology.

FROM THE DEEP WEB TO THE DARK WEB

The Deep Web

The deep web essentially existed on the early Internet due to username/password blocks. The basic mechanism to protect information on the early web was to put it behind an authentication wall. You may recall from chapter 1 that any information or sites located behind an authentication wall, or a paywall, are part of what is considered the deep web. As the network grew larger, more sites and information were located behind authentication walls. When commercial sites joined, the deep web grew larger as they started putting information and resources behind paywalls. When search engines started to create indexes of all the pages they could reach, the deep web grew larger still as organizations and groups started putting information in places where it could not be reached by search engines.

The term *deep web* did not exist until a computer scientist named Michael K. Bergman coined it in 2001. He is generally credited with creating the term in a paper he published on searching the Internet.[11] He estimated that in the year 2000, the surface web contained around one billion individual documents and pages, and that the deep web was around 550 billion. Current estimates put the surface web at around 4.5 billion pages. If the general estimates of how much larger the deep web is compared to the surface web are true, that would mean the deep web is currently around two to three trillion pages—equal to about 400 pages for each person in the world, or about 1,000 pages for each person worldwide who has regular access to the Internet. Keep in mind that this is purely an estimation since it is not known with any degree of certainty how much is on the deep web.[12]

THE BIRTH OF THE
INTERNET AND DARK WEB: A TIMELINE

October 1969: First two ARPANET nodes are connected between UCLA and SRI International in Menlo Park (San Francisco), California

December 1971: Fifteen sites across the United States are connected via ARPANET

Fall 1973: Networks connect to several major research universities in United Kingdom

July 1979: Internet Architecture Board, which provides oversight to the development of the Internet, is established

March 1985: Symbolics.com, the first .com domain name, is registered by Symbolics, Inc.

November 1985: America Online (AOL) services launch

November 1989: The World is established as the first major commercial Internet service provider in the United States

December 1990: Tim Berners-Lee releases the first web browser, called WorldWideWeb, and the first website

September 1993: W3Catalog, the first Internet search engine, is made available to the public

July 1995: Amazon.com opens to the public as an online bookseller

September 1995: Ebay.com launches

September 1998: Google.com launches

March 2000: Initial launch of Freenet anonymous web project

January 2001: Wikipedia.org launches

September 2002: Tor Project is released for public use

August 2003: Start of development of I2P anonymous web platform

February 2004: Facebook.com launches

As time passed, the Internet continued to grow, and as the deep web became deeper, many people started to see the need for going dark. People were using the Internet for private communication. It began to be used by those members of our society who wanted or needed a greater level of protection from those who would want to silence them. Corporations and governments began to monitor and watch what people were doing on the Internet, and in some cases, to block them.

Take, for example, governments like China that attempt to filter the Internet communication coming in and out of the country. In 1994 the Internet was introduced to the country of China. The president at the time, Jiang Zemin, believed that the Internet was a crucial necessity to move China from an industrialized nation into an informational nation. He believed that the Internet would bolster the country's competitive edge in an advancing worldwide market. Almost immediately, it became apparent to the officials of the country that allowing the "Western ideals" of other nations to come into the country would expose their citizens to ideas and beliefs that they did not agree with. In 2000 the Chinese government instituted the Golden Shield project, which was designed to give control of the flow of information to the government, to protect the citizens from what the government felt was inappropriate. This project did work, but it created a culture in China of censorship. All activities on the Internet in China were subject to censorship by the government. Even companies (like Google and Yahoo) that wish to do business in China must abide by these censorship rules and block all information deemed unacceptable.[13]

As the Internet became more commercially viable, businesses saw the opportunity to expand their sales base to a wider market. The Internet also created new revenue streams that were not available before. Companies started putting ads on other websites to promote their products or services. These banner ads started appearing in 1994. They were initially innocuous ads that simply wanted to be clicked on to send a user to their site. They often used funny or catchy graphics to entice the user to click on them. One early AT&T banner ad drew an impressive 44 percent click rate.[14] But as people began to get used to banner ads and the click rate decreased, the marketers attempted new strategies. Some companies developed ways to target ads to consumers. Instead of just placing ads on every web page they could to reach as many users as they could, they attempted to find ways to make the ads relevant to the user.

WebConnect was an Internet advertising company that allowed their clients to place ads on their pages that directed at the users. The way they did this, however, was a manual process. Each client would have to manually place the ads. Other companies like Doubleclick offered more directed and targeted ad placement by tracking user behavior and analytics. This allowed them to more efficiently place ads and therefore generate higher revenue. Online marketing became less effective as Internet users got used to targeted ads, so the marketers developed pop-up and pop-under ads. These were small Internet pages that were launched automatically when a page was visited. They would remain open even after a user navigated away from the launching page, and even after the main browser window was closed. The pop-up window would launch on top of the current page, and the pop-under window would launch behind the current page. Pop-up and pop-under ads did not last long, but they showed the ability of Internet advertisers to find new ways to target ads to users.

Internet cookies also became a popular way for companies to target ads to users. A cookie is a small text file on the user's computer that can store information about the user's movements on the Internet, or their usage of a particular site. When a user visits a particular site, a cookie can be placed on the user's computer that keeps track of what the user did on that site. It remembers what they viewed, what they clicked on, and how long they were there. Some cookies stay on the computer even after the user has left that site. If the cookie is a third-party cookie, or a cookie that originates from a different company than the one the user was visiting, then the third party will gain knowledge of the user's behavior across multiple sites. If that third party is an advertising company, it can monitor a user's activities across the Internet, and then target ads to them based on their history. Cookies still exist today, and have only increased in complexity and their ability to be useful to marketers.

Even the United States government was tracking and recording what people did on the Internet. Before the Internet, the National Security Agency (NSA) was on ARPANET and was responsible for routing information that crossed its connections. As ARPANET grew and more nongovernment links were created, the NSA fought hard to keep encryption in its hands, and attempted to block any attempts to use encryption that it could not decrypt. The NSA continued to track users across the network and eventually created ways to collect, store, and use the traffic on the Internet.

A FEW MAJOR CONTRIBUTORS TO THE DEVELOPMENT OF THE INTERNET AND THE DARK WEB

Leonard Kleinrock (b. 1934), Paul Baran (1926–2011), Donald Davies (1924–2000), and Lawrence Roberts (b. 1937) developed the concept of packet switching, which was influential on the development of ARPANET, the forerunner of the modern Internet. Roberts was manager of ARPANET project while at the Advanced Research Projects Agency.

Tim Berners-Lee (b. 1955) is the creator of the World Wide Web (www) and Hypertext Transfer Protocol (http), which made the modern Internet possible. Rather than patent his protocol, which surely would have made him the wealthiest person alive today, he sees the Internet as a force for good and works to make it available to all.

Paul Syverson, Michael Reed, and David Goldschlag of the Naval Research Laboratory were responsible for the development of onion routing and the Onion Router (Tor).

Ian Clarke at the University of Edinburgh wrote a report entitled "A Distributed Decentralised Information Storage and Retrieval System" and later cowrote "Freenet: A Distributed Anonymous Information Storage and Retrieval System." These writings served as the foundation of the Freenet platform discussed in this book. Clarke remains connected to Freenet (including occasionally responding to email queries about the platform).

After the attacks on the World Trade Center in 2001, the United States government passed new regulations that allowed it to create new surveillance programs to monitor the Internet use of foreign and American citizens. The USA Patriot Act was passed by Congress in 2001 and continues to have an impact on the Internet. It granted government agencies more power to collect and store more Internet traffic than they ever could before. It traded privacy for the promise of increased safety for America's citizens.[15]

In 2013 a contractor for the CIA and the NSA named Edward Snowden revealed a wealth of internal documents from the NSA that exposed the technologies the agency used to monitor the Internet. Among them was PRISM, a surveillance program designed by the NSA that collects and stores Internet traffic from United States Internet companies like Google, Yahoo, and Verizon. He also released details of other governments involved in Internet tracking and surveillance. For example, Tempora is a program used by the British government to collect, store, and utilize Internet traffic. He also exposed a system of government payments to purchase information from Internet providers, attempts by the government to recruit informants from online communities, and the extent to which the United States government was surveilling other countries, including Brazil, France, Mexico, Britain, China, Germany, and Spain.[16]

Safety began to be an issue on the Internet as well. Internet attacks, or cyberattacks, started to grow as the Internet expanded. There are a variety of ways people can be attacked on the Internet. The most common are viruses and spyware, but some attacks are more malicious. Sometimes, people, organizations, or governments will use the Internet to seek out other individuals or organizations to steal from or attack. Many times attacks are targeted at individuals to gain access to financial information, or at businesses to gain access to corporate information. In the late 1990s Internet worms, or self-replicating viruses, spread across the Internet, causing slowdowns and wreaking havoc in corporations and governments. One of the worst was released in 2000. It was called the ILOVEYOU worm, and within hours of its release it had spread across the world. It is estimated that, within days, more than fifty million infections were reported worldwide. The financial impact of the ILOVEYOU worm is estimated at $15 billion.[17]

The Internet became a hotspot for politically motivated manipulation as a result of its ubiquity in the developed world. Extremist groups could use it to manipulate individuals into joining their cause and governments could distribute false information and influence public perceptions (such as with the 2016 United States elections).

Deeper Still

The Internet was now a major communication platform, spanning the entire world and reaching hundreds of millions of users. Individuals, companies, and governments relied on the Internet to distribute information and knowledge, but as the Internet grew, so did the desire to control it. Governments wanted to prevent their citizens from learning about the world, and prevent the rest of the world from knowing about them. Companies wanted to find new revenue streams from the wealth of information about people on the Internet. Individuals wanted to steal or disrupt the communication that occurred. People wanted and needed ways to use the Internet that were not monitored or tracked. They desired ways to explore and discover without the fear of filtering or surveillance. Enter the dark web.

TOR

Tor originally started out as a project by the United States Naval Research Laboratory in the mid-1990s.[18] It was initially called the Onion Router and was later shortened to just Tor. It got its name from the way the network routes the traffic, creating layers of encryption over the transmission packets similar to the way onions have layers. The Naval Research Laboratory was attempting to find a way to create protected communication on the Internet for government intelligence activities. In 1997 the

Defense Advanced Research Projects Agency (DARPA) further developed the Tor project to create the first release in 2002. In 2004 the Naval Research Laboratory released the code for the Tor project to the public for free. The Electronic Frontier Foundation (EFF) continued funding the project's original creators, Roger Dingledine and Nick Mathewson. They later founded the Tor Project, a 501(c)(3) research educational organization responsible for maintaining Tor. Initially, the major financial backer of the Tor Project was the United States government, along with many other organizations interested in creating Internet privacy.

THE BIRTH OF A DARK WEB NETWORK

The Onion Router (Tor) has grown into the most popular dark web browser, with millions of daily users, but started far from the public's purview. Instead, it grew and evolved into the public sphere the same way most major communication technologies do, through development by the United States government, enacted to benefit the nation's defense. The telegraph was expanded during the American Civil War to facilitate communication among troops. World War I sparked the development of the radio. World War II saw the development of encoding machines that were the predecessors of the computer. The Cold War sparked the development of what would become the Internet. Tor was simply the latest communication technology to be developed to support the nation's defense. Communication technology and military defense are intimately linked. Regardless of your opinion of the military and war, it is likely that many of these technologies never would have been developed if it was not for the purpose of gaining a strategic advantage over military foes.

In the release of information from Snowden, he revealed plans by the NSA to expose Tor users and infiltrate their communication. The agency attempted to identify users on the Tor network and then use a special type of redirection to point their communication to the NSA servers. Once the NSA was watching the traffic, it could infect a user's computer with a special application that deanonymized their communication. Since this revelation, the NSA is purported to have stopped this infection.

Tor has grown since its inception to be one of the most frequently used dark web tools. Recent studies have put the number of people using Tor daily at around six million. It has gathered a lot of press with illegal ventures like Silk Road, which offered a variety of illegal products for sale (discussed thoroughly in chapter 7), but it has also been promoted as a privacy tool that is used by a large variety of people. Snowden himself is known to use the Tor network for his communications.

Communication is a necessary part of human existence. We have always sought ways to communicate faster and more efficiently. It only made sense that as computer technology grew and we started using it more, we would start seeing ways to make it communicate better. The United States government saw a chance to create more efficient communication between government agencies across the nation. Eventually, educational institutions joined up, and then the general public. As the Internet grew and became a global communication tool, some people sought to exploit that tool for their own needs. Money began to be involved, and governments wanted more control. Out of necessity, a dark web began to grow that offered a way to combat the loss of privacy, lack of anonymity, and loss of control. The dark web was born.

FREENET

In 1999 a student at the University of Edinburgh named Ian Clarke published a graduation paper titled "A Distributed Decentralised Information Storage and Retrieval System." As a result of that paper, a group of researchers, including Clarke, published a paper called "Freenet: A Distributed Anonymous Information Storage and Retrieval System" in 2001.[19] The abstract summarizes the purpose of the paper, how Freenet operates, and the benefits quite nicely:

> We describe Freenet, an adaptive peer-to-peer network application that permits the publication, replication, and retrieval of data while protecting the anonymity of both authors and readers. Freenet operates as a network of identical nodes that collectively pool their storage space to store data files and cooperate to route requests to the most likely physical location of data. No broadcast search or centralized location index is employed. Files are referred to in a location-independent manner, and are dynamically replicated in locations near requesters and deleted from locations where there is no interest. It is infeasible to discover the true origin or destination of a file passing through the network, and difficult for a node operator to determine or be held responsible for the actual physical contents of her own node.[20]

Some of this may sound confusing, but we will cover more of the "how" in chapter 3. Right now, understand that they created Freenet to solve what they observed as some faults in the Internet—mainly the lack of privacy for users, and the storage of data in only a few locations, thus creating a single point of failure. In the paper, they laid out five design goals for Freenet:

1. Anonymity for both producers and consumers of information
2. Deniability for storers of information
3. Resistance to attempts by third parties to deny access to information
4. Efficient dynamic storage and routing of information
5. Decentralization of all network functions

I2P

I2P, or the Invisible Internet Project, was started in 2003 by a group of volunteers who wanted to create an encrypted path across the Internet for the purpose of censorship-resistant communication. The I2P network was designed to offer the option of anonymity to activists, oppressed people, journalists, whistleblowers, and average Internet users. Though it was the last of the major three dark web platforms to emerge, it helped to push research into anonymous networks forward, bringing the dark web front and center in the public sphere.

NOTES

1. Alan M. Turing, "On Computable Numbers, with an Application to the Entscheidungsproblem," *Proceedings of the London Mathematical Society* 42, no. 1 (1936): 230–65, https://www.cs.virginia.edu/~robins/Turing_Paper_1936.pdf.

2. Vannevar Bush, "As We May Think," *Atlantic*, July 1945, https://www.theatlantic.com/magazine/archive/1945/07/as-we-may-think/303881/.

3. James M. Nyce and Paul Kahn, *From Memex to Hypertext: Vannevar Bush and the Mind's Machine* (Boston: Academic Press, 1991).

4. Claude E. Shannon, "A Mathematical Theory of Communication," *Bell System Technical Journal* 27, no. 3 (1948): 379–423.

5. Claude E. Shannon and Warren Weaver, *The Mathematical Theory of Communication* (Urbana: University of Illinois Press, 1949).

6. Lawrence G. Roberts, "The Evolution of Packet Switching," November 1978, http://www.packet.cc/files/ev-packet-sw.html.

7. Barry M. Leiner, Vinton G. Cerf, David D. Clark, Robert E. Kahn, Leonard Kleinrock, Daniel C. Lynch, Jon Postel, Larry G. Roberts, and Stephen Wolff, "Brief History of the Internet," Internet Society, 1997, https://www.internetsociety.org/internet/history-internet/brief-history-internet/#f5.

8. Margaret Rouse, "ARPANET," TechTarget.com, March 2017, https://searchnetworking.techtarget.com/definition/ARPANET.

9. National Science Foundation, "A Brief History of NSF and the Internet," accessed August 28, 2018, https://www.nsf.gov/news/special_reports/cyber/internet.jsp.

10. Susan W. Brenner, *Cybercrime and the Law: Challenges, Issues, and Outcomes* (Boston: Northeastern University Press, 2012).

11. Michael K. Bergman, "The Deep Web: Surfacing Hidden Value," *Journal of Electronic Publishing* 7, no. 1 (2001).

12. Michael Chertoff, "A Public Policy Perspective of the Dark Web," *Journal of Cyber Policy* 2, no. 1 (2017): 26–38, https://doi.org/10.1080/23738871.2017.1298643.

13. Ping Punyakumpol, "The Great Firewall of China: Background," Torfox, June 1, 2001, https://cs.stanford.edu/people/eroberts/cs201/projects/2010-11/FreedomOfInformationChina/category/great-firewall-of-china/index.html.

14. Karla Cook, "A Brief History of Online Advertising," *HubSpot* (blog), September 12, 2016, https://blog.hubspot.com/marketing/history-of-online-advertising.

15. US Department of Justice, "The USA PATRIOT Act: Preserving Life and Liberty," accessed August 23, 2018, https://www.justice.gov/archive/ll/highlights.htm.

16. Ewen MacAskill and Gabriel Dance, "NSA Files: Decoded," *Guardian*, November 1, 2013, https://www.theguardian.com/world/interactive/2013/nov/01/snowden-nsa-files -surveillance-revelations-decoded#section/1.

17. Jon Martindale, "From Pranks to Nuclear Sabotage, This Is the History of Malware," Digital Trends, March 29, 2018, https://www.digitaltrends.com/computing/history-of -malware/.

18. DarkOwl, "Darknet Series: A Brief History of Tor," September 1, 2016, https://www .darkowl.com/blog/2016/6/21/darknet-series-a-brief-history-of-tor.

19. Ian Clarke, Oskar Sandberg, Brandon Wiley, and Theodore W. Hong, "Freenet: A Distributed Anonymous Information Storage and Retrieval System," *Proceedings of the International Workshop on Designing Privacy Enhancing Technologies: Design Issues in Anonymity and Unobservability*, ed. Hannes Federrath, (Berlin: Springer, 2001), 46–66.

20. Ibid.

3

How It Works: The Dark Details

In chapter 2, we learned the basics of how the Internet works. Devices on the Internet "network" pass packets of information around and route them to their destination. We also learned a bit about how the deep web and the dark web work. In this chapter let us dive in deeper and gain a fuller understanding of how the dark web works. Having this basic understanding will help to illustrate why the dark web is a necessary extension to the Internet, and how it protects privacy. We will also dig deeper into the ways the individual applications—I2P, Freenet, and Tor—work.

UNDERSTANDING THE INTERNET

At its simplest, the Internet is really just a stream of data (1s and 0s). Envision a flowing river. Each molecule of water in the river is a packet of information moving from one place to another. Of course, our Internet river is a two-way stream. Data can pass up the river just as easily as down. Each packet of data was put on the river by a device with an address attached to it. The address is usually a set of numbers called an IP address that tells the packet where to go. For example, if you send a search request to www.google.com, you are really sending packets of information to the Internet protocol (IP) address for Google. Once the packet is put on the river, it is routed around the Internet by routers and other servers until it reaches the destination device. The destination device puts all the packets of information back together and reads the message. If it needs to, it will then put together a series of packets in response back to you. This all happens very quickly and rarely involves any problems. There are all kinds of methods in place to make sure that packets are routed correctly, and that the packets are not corrupted during their travels. These things do happen from time to time, but the systems that send and receive packets are quite adept at fixing them.

WHAT IS AN IP ADDRESS?

IP stands for Internet protocol. An IP address is used to uniquely identify a device on a network. Without an IP address, the device would not be able to send or receive any information.

Think of an IP as a postal address. If someone is mailing you a box, they must know your postal address. An IP address is the same: if someone wants to send you information on the network, they must know your IP address.

A typical IP address is in the format of four sets of numbers ranging between 0 and 255. They look similar to this: 192.169.1.44. With this combination of numbers, it is possible to have up to 4,294,967,296 addresses.

With the increase in devices connecting to the Internet and needing IP addresses, a new standard is coming into play called IP V6 that has more addresses. An IP V6 address looks like this: 1203:8fe0:fe80:b897:8990:8a7c:99bf:323d. With this longer string, it is possible to have up to 340,282,366,920, 938,463,463,374,607,431,768,211,456 unique addresses.

Now imagine an Internet provider. It supplies a path to the river for a set of people. All the packets of information that its users send or receive pass through its servers for routing. The Internet provider servers can, and often do, keep track of the places the users go. Think of it this way: a computer on the Internet provider's service makes a request for www.google.com to search for "luggage." As that request is passed through the servers at the Internet provider, a log is created showing the date, time, who accessed that site, and what they did on the site. This information can be stored for any period of time, so that a complete record of all the things a particular user does on the Internet is kept, and could be recalled if needed.

WHAT IS AN INTERNET SERVICE PROVIDER?

An Internet service provider serves as the facilitator between the local Internet network (the router and modem, and your laptops, desktops, and mobile devices) and the servers of the websites you want to access. It controls who and how the "river" flows between users and websites. For the majority of the public Internet's history, Internet service providers generally sent connections down the river on a first come, first served basis and kept the river at a steady flow. With the end of net neutrality, that may potentially change. Internet service providers could send five of one person's connection requests while only sending one of another's requests over that same period, based on who is willing to pay more. Similarly, it may be possible for certain sites to make agreements with Internet service providers that would speed up access to their site and slow it down for competitors. The end of net neutrality essentially enables Internet service providers to build as many virtual dams as they want.

Think about the Internet services as well. Google can and does keep a record of all the searches made on its site. It does this for a variety of reasons. It uses the information to refine its search process and make it more useful. It also uses this data to sell to advertisers, or for its own advertising purposes. Some of this data is stripped of personally identifiable information, but not always.[1] Remember Edward Snowden, discussed in the previous chapter? One of his leaks was in regards to certain Internet providers and Internet systems releasing information about their users in bulk. The program was called PRISM and was designed to allow the NSA to demand, collect, and analyze Internet traffic from users. The agency requested data from many corporations, including Microsoft, Yahoo, Google, Facebook, AOL, Skype, YouTube, and Apple.[2]

THE DARK WEB

As discussed earlier, in the early 2000s the dark web began to grow at the depths of the deep web in response to the continuing lack of privacy and security that the open Internet offered. Several applications appeared, each with its own intent and way of operating. They all shared the same ideal: find a way to grant users some level of privacy or anonymity on the Internet. Let us take a look at each of the major applications and understand how they work.

WHAT'S IN A NAME? DARK WEB TERMINOLOGY

From *dark web* to Tor to I2P, there are many terms discussed in this book that appear to have very technical or insidious names but are, in fact, quite descriptive. *Dark web* describes the fact that those trying to track you in the network will be left in the dark. "Tor is the acronym for the Onion Router, named because, like onions, this router (connector) has layers (that preserve anonymity). I2P is the acronym for the Invisible Internet Project. Invisible Internet should seem pretty self-explanatory in the context of enhanced privacy—it makes you "invisible" on the Internet. Freenet, well, makes you free from unwanted surveillance.

I2P

As discussed earlier, I2P is a network on top of the Internet that uses encryption and a form of tunneling to protect communication. It creates a layer of connections between devices on I2P. Each device on the layer acts as a "node," a point along the route that the information travels. [3]

When I2P is installed, it creates a router on your computer. This router connects to other routers on the I2P network. The connection to each router on the network is called a tunnel. The tunnels are encrypted with several layers of encryption so that each router on the network is not able to unpack and read the data in the tunnel. There are two kinds of tunnels passing through routers: inbound and outbound tunnels. The first device on a tunnel is called the gateway tunnel.

The inbound tunnel receives the packet from the peer, then forwards it along the created tunnel by using the outbound tunnel. The outbound tunnel encodes the message with more encryption, and then sends it out to the next node.

Each tunnel has two endpoints: the first is the creator of the tunnel, and the last is the final router on the tunnel. Once a message is received at the last router on the tunnel, it is not necessarily at its final destination. Depending on the routing, it might be pushed down another tunnel before it reaches its final stop.

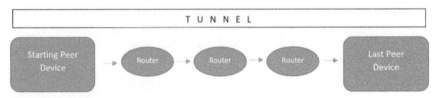

Figure 3.1. Diagram of I2P Tunnel

Each router on the network creates a series of inbound and outbound tunnels that can be used by other nodes on the network. When a router receives a request from a peer to use a tunnel, it gathers the communication, adds a layer of encryption, and pushes it down its tunnel.

Once a communication reaches its final router, it is decrypted and pushed to the application. So, how does the I2P routing software know where to send messages, and how does it create tunnels? It uses a specialized database called the netdb, or network database. It is a collection of all the tunnel gateways and routers available. When a router wants to use a tunnel, it contacts the netdb and obtains the contact information for a router. It then contacts that router to get references for other routers. It contacts the other routers and learns more about routers connected to them. From this list of information, the peer device creates its own database of routers.

I2P has many applications developed to work on its network. File sharing applications like BitTorrent and eMule can be directed to use the I2P network. There are also several email and chat applications like I2P-Bote and I2P-Messenger that were developed for use on I2P.

Freenet

The designers of Freenet wanted a safe, secure, and private way to communicate on the Internet that was free from censorship.[4] The goal was to create an environment for file sharing, publishing, and other forms of communication. The idea was to create a way for information to be stored so that it was not possible to determine who posted the information, and to make it difficult to block or remove information from the system. Freenet accomplishes these goals by creating a distributed storage system.

For Freenet to operate, each computer on the network must be connected with the Freenet client. In this case, the Freenet client is an application that is installed on the computer and creates the connection to the Freenet network. Once the client is installed, it becomes a node on the network. Each node has an amount of space set aside for storage. This storage becomes a part of the Freenet network. When the node connects to the network, it creates connections to the nearest nodes to it, and creates a store of these known nodes. Since each node is aware of other nodes, a virtual map is created, but each node is aware of only the nodes nearest it. No single node is aware of the entire network. As information is routed from node to node, each node just passes it to the next node on its list. If that node does not contain the information that was requested, it sends back a failure. The first node then tries a different node. This keeps happening until a timeout is received or the information is located. If it is located, the data is then routed back through the nodes to the original requester.

Let us take a look at a typical request. In figure 3.2, you can see node A requesting some information. Using its own node database, it sends a request (1) to node B for the information. Node B does not have it, so it sends the request (2) to node C.

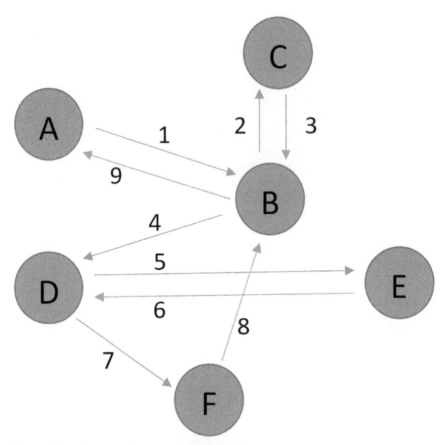

Figure 3.2.   Diagram of Freenet Communication

Node C does not have it, so it sends back a failure (3). Node B then tries again to node D (4). Node D does not have the information, so it tries node E from its own database (5). Node E does not have it, so it sends back a failure (6). Node D tries node F (7). Node F does have the information that node A wants, so it sends the information back to node B (8), which sends it back to node A (9). This whole process continues until node A has all the information it requested and displays it to the user.

The Freenet network distributes information to multiple nodes. No single node contains all the blocks necessary to reconstruct a file, as that file is broken up and stored all over in different nodes. When a client application requests a particular file, it queries the network, and starts connecting to nodes to locate the pieces of the file and then reassembles them. When a client inserts a file into the network, the same procedure is used, except that it places pieces of the file on other nodes instead of requesting them.

Each node on the path will use a type of encryption designed to protect the communication and to facilitate the transfer of data between nodes. Files are stored on the network using a key-based lookup service. Basically, each file on the network is given a unique key that points to itself. The key is generated by hashing the file. A hash is a text file that is generated by running the file through a hash table that creates values based on the content. Once this hash is created, it is then assigned to the Freenet system as a key. This is a useful way to store information about files since the hash is unique to each file. Using the key-based system, when a request is made for a document, the system uses the key to narrow down the likely location of the file since similar keys tend to be stored near each other on nodes. The nodes themselves keep track of the keys, forming a type of caching request system that reduces the time it takes to locate and retrieve the files. The keys and hashes also create a foundation for the encryption used to protect the data itself.

Freenet offers users two different types of networking based on their needs. The opennet feature of Freenet is the default configuration and uses public nodes that connect to other nodes. Using this system, nodes are constantly communicating with each other, and when requests are made for content, they connect to other nodes without any intervention by the user. This is the most efficient and easy way to use the Freenet network, but it can leave nodes open to attack by intruders or foreign governments. The other option, darknet, is much more secure. With the darknet feature turned on, users connect only to other nodes they are familiar with and trust. This is basically creating a network within the Freenet network. Using this configuration is the most secure and private way of communicating with Freenet.

The way the Freenet network operates allows the easy distribution of information on the network in an anonymous way. Once a document or other type of information is placed on the network, the person who placed it there can disconnect and not be associated with that information any further. This is how the high level of anonymity is created. Also, once the information is on the network, no one person owns it or is responsible for it. It is taken apart and distributed across the network in multiple locations. This also allows for increased redundancy. If a node crashes or is removed from the network, the information it contained is not lost. Other nodes will have copies of the data, and clients requesting the information will be able to locate it. There is also increased data protection. When the key is generated, it is based on the hash of the file. If the file is modified or changed in a way that it should not be, the key that is generated will be different. The system will know that the file has been modified and adapt by getting a new copy of it.

Tor

Tor is the most popular dark web tool available. It owes much of its popularity to the way it operates and the connections it offers. Like other dark web tools (such as I2P and Freenet), Tor offers information and links that are internal to itself and not available off the Tor network, but it also offers an easy way to connect to surface websites in a way that ensures a lot of anonymity.

Tor uses a routing system called onion routing. Remember that Tor originally stood for the Onion Router, which was named after the way information is moved around the Tor network. Onions have layers and so does onion routing. Onion routing works by taking a packet of information and applying layers of encryption to it. The packet is then sent into the Tor network and to another relay. At that relay, a layer of the encryption is removed and the packet is then passed to another relay. As the packet of information is passed from relay to relay, layers of encryption are removed. Eventually, the packet of information has enough of its layers removed and the packet exits the Tor network to the surface web, or retrieves the information from the Tor site it requested.

Let us take a look at a typical communication on the Tor network. The user wants to access a server on the surface web using the Tor network. The Tor client on User A's computer packages up the request in several layers of encryption and then sends it to a relay on the network (1). The client gathers a list of the nodes nearby from a directory it receives when it connects to the network. When the client encrypts the request, the top layer of encryption is encoded for the first relay. When that relay accepts the request, it decrypts the topmost layer and reads the next layer, which tells it where to route the packet next. It uses the next relay's information to add another layer before sending the packet to the next relay (2). That relay does the same thing: decrypt the layer meant for it, read where it is supposed to send the request next, then encrypt it again and send it on (3–6). Eventually, based on the original layers in the request, it reaches the final relay. That relay then decrypts the final layer on the request and routes it to the surface web (7). In some cases, the request will stay on the Tor network in the form of an .onion website. In this situation, it stays on the network. When the request is sent back to the client, it follows a similar reverse path, except the routing from relay to relay is created by the original exit node back to the client.

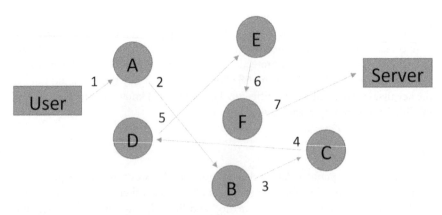

Figure 3.3. Diagram of Tor Communication

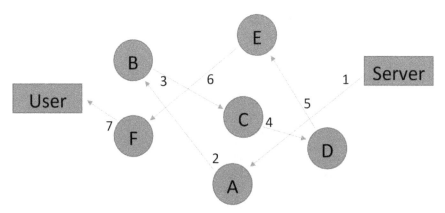

Figure 3.4. Tor Communication Reverse Path

The client will continue to use the same relay path through the network for a random amount of time, and then switch to another randomly generated path. This randomness creates a difficult situation for anyone wanting to watch or monitor the traffic originating from or returning to a client. Since relays can come and go on the network, the same path is never used again, so capturing the information is nearly impossible.

There are several types of applications that can be used on the Tor network. The most obvious is an Internet browser like Firefox or Chrome. Each can be configured to use the Tor network by installing the Tor application on the computer and then redirecting the browser using a proxy connection. Tor also offers a prebuilt version of the Firefox browser that is configured to use the Tor network automatically. There are also chat applications developed or implemented on the Tor. File sharing applications like Vuze and BitTorrent can be used on the Tor network.

CONCLUSION

The Internet was developed to be open and free. The technologies that run the Internet were not initially developed to provide privacy or anonymity. As the need grew to increase this privacy on the Internet, the dark web began to emerge. New technologies were designed to work under or on top of the existing Internet. In other words, the designers of the dark web figured out ways to use the surface web to provide what it was not designed to do. Many types of dark web tools were created, each with their own purpose and design. I2P was created to allow people to communicate quickly in an anonymous way. It uses a tunneling protocol that creates secure and encrypted paths around the Internet. Freenet was designed to be a distributed network on top of the Internet that allows the publishing of anonymous information that is safe from censorship. Tor was created to send encrypted and private communication to the surface web and to dark web sites on its network. While all three applications provide a way to enter the dark web, each does it differently. Each has its own special way to provide privacy and anonymity.

NOTES

1. Google, "Data Transparency," accessed September 18, 2018, https://safety.google/privacy/data/.

2. Barton Gellman and Laura Poitras, "US, British Intelligence Mining Data from Nine US Internet Companies in Broad Secret Program," *Washington Post*, June 7, 2013, https://www.washingtonpost.com/investigations/us-intelligence-mining-data-from-nine-us-internet-companies-in-broad-secret-program/2013/06/06/3a0c0da8-cebf-11e2-8845-d970ccb04497_story.html.

3. The Invisible Internet Project, "I2P: A Scalable Framework for Anonymous Communication," accessed September 18, 2018, https://geti2p.net/en/docs/how/tech-intro.

4. Ian Clarke, Oskar Sandberg, Brandon Wiley, and Theodore W. Hong, "Freenet: A Distributed Anonymous Information Storage and Retrieval System," *Proceedings of the International Workshop on Designing Privacy Enhancing Technologies: Design Issues in Anonymity and Unobservability*, ed. Hannes Federrath, (Berlin: Springer, 2001), 46–66.

4

Distinguishing Fact from Fiction:
Is the Dark Web Really Dark?

HOW DO WE DEFINE THE DARK WEB?

It is important to understand the etymology of the word *dark* in the term *dark web*. *Dark* is not intended to be used in the context of "evil or nefarious," but rather in the context of "having no light or clarity," or "unknown or obscure." The term *dark web* refers to a web platform in which the identity of users is obscured.[1] The easy application of the term in its nefarious context is unfortunate and likely what has caused the dark web to garner such a troublesome reputation in popular culture. It is not uncommon for us to misappropriate computer terminology and its history. Many of us, for instance, do not realize that *email* is short for "electronic mail" or that Amazon started as an online used bookstore before growing into the trillion-dollar corporation it is today. However, the dark web, unlike the former examples, has its reputation detrimentally impacted by this misunderstanding of the term's meaning and origin.

The false definition plays right into narratives that media and organizations like to foster to drive clicks. This is why some users and supporters of the dark web have taken to referring to the service by the name of the browser they use (e.g., "I support Tor"), or using the term *anonymous web* (which we recommend).[2] This terminology turns the idea of the dark web on its head by not only suggesting a benefit (anonymity) to the service, but also suggesting that the regular Internet is not anonymous (which is absolutely true). While it may be hard to believe that just the words we use can have a major impact on how an object or idea is perceived, consider how long, for instance, we think about what to name our child (or dog or cat, for that matter) or a new product, or what words we say when communicating with a colleague. Names matter. The dark web has an unfortunate one.

That is not to say that the dark web is squeaky clean. There is illegal content on the dark web—but there is also illegal content on the regular web.[3] In fact, while the dark web may proportionally have more illegal content, the regular web, being as large as it is, is likely to have far more illegal content in sheer quantity. There is nothing in the regular or dark web that can prevent illegal content from being uploaded. It is not as though if one uploads illegal content to a GoDaddy server a message pops up that reads "Nope! That's not allowed!" Simply put, the Internet is policed so that illegal content can be taken down and the perpetrators apprehended. This is true of the dark web also, as we will discuss in chapter 7; it is just a more difficult process to shut down a site.

Many of the sites on the dark web that have been the target of media reports are sites that have long existed on the regular Internet. The Pirate Bay, Farmer's Market, and Library Genesis are responsible for distributing copyrighted materials and illicit drugs worth hundreds of millions of dollars each year. All three of these sites started on the regular Internet.[4] While the Pirate Bay and Farmer's Market are now defunct on all platforms, Library Genesis still exists on the regular Internet (its .com domain was revoked, but its .io domain remains functional) as well as on the dark web. This site provides millions of copyrighted books and articles free of charge, which led to a lawsuit from Elsevier and allied publishers but did not stop the site from being available to the public. Illegal content is everywhere on the web, if you look for it (which we are not advocating).[5]

Let us explore some common myths about the dark web and the extent to which they are or are not factual. Many of these myths will be discussed in greater detail in the following chapters.

MYTH 1: THE DARK WEB IS THE PLACE WHERE TERRORISTS GO TO BUY WEAPONS AND PLAN ATTACKS

Reality: While it is certainly possible that some terrorist groups use the dark web, it is not a rampant phenomenon that you will inevitably run into as a casual dark web user.

Many terrorist organizations have much more brazen techniques than hanging out on the anonymous web. For instance, the Islamic State of Iraq and the Levant (ISIL/ISIS) was known for creating fake accounts on popular social media sites to recruit new members. In the 2016 United States elections, Russian operatives used regular email addresses to coordinate movements and conducted several overt acts on major social media sites.[6] While there are far too many tragic acts of terrorism and mass violence in the United States, there are still relatively few compared to what some media outlets will make it seem and most acts are perpetrated by a lone individual who acquired information and tools not from the dark web but rather the Internet and around their own home or legally from gun shows and hardware stores. It would be nice to believe that all terrorist activity is coordinated in this one network because we could believe that all we have to do is shut it down and everything in the world would be okay. Unfortunately, the reality is far more complex than these narratives make you believe. We cannot simply blame all the world's problems on the Internet (or dark web).

MYTH 2: THE DARK WEB IS MOSTLY A MARKETPLACE FOR ILLICIT DRUGS

Reality: There are drug sales on the dark web. However, they are not as rampant as they are made to seem. Many of the sites you read about in the media—and these are "real" sites you can visit if you have dark web software—are hoaxes or scams.[7] They might be created as a joke, or to actually get your money, but there are no drugs being exchanged. How would the seller get such drugs to you? Send them via USPS? Even if they did, how is this supposed to occur without compromising your anonymity, which is supposedly the whole point of buying drugs on the dark web? How could a buyer feel certain that the site was not actually created by the government? The site most known for illegal transactions on the dark web was Silk Road (which will be discussed in greater detail in chapters 6 and 7). At the time of the site's closing, it was suggested in the FBI's complaint that 147,000 buyers worldwide had used the site since its inception three years earlier. That is slightly more than one-tenth the total number of drug possession violations in the United States in 2017 alone, or 0.002 percent of all drug users worldwide during that period (729 million from 2011 to 2013), according to the United Nations Office on Drugs and Crime.[8] So while illegal drug trade did exist on the dark web, the problem was and is much bigger than the dark web and will not be solved by banning the dark web.

MYTH 3: THE DARK WEB HAS NO VALUE TO AN "UPSTANDING" CITIZEN

Reality: We hope that this book demonstrates this is not the case. If we, the authors, truly believed that there was no value of the dark web for the average person, we would not be writing this book. On the contrary, we see very few differences between the dark web and the regular Internet you are accustomed to using as far as changes in user experience go (the dark web, after all, is built on the same bare bones as the regular Internet) but immense benefit in increased privacy. Even if you feel you do not need privacy, your support helps those who do.

Unfortunately, humans are predisposed to be untrusting of the unfamiliar. Again, we hope this book helps abate that disposition. We want the dark web to be something that people feel comfortable about and proud advocating for in their communities. Your voice is key to ensuring that this resource remains viable for those who need it.

MYTH 4: IT IS ILLEGAL TO USE THE DARK WEB

Reality: Using the dark web is definitely *not* a crime (at least not in the United States).[9] In fact, we (the authors of the book) use the dark web regularly at work and for personal use. Criminalizing use of the dark web would be like criminalizing standing in an alley. Do illegal trades occur in alleys? Yes. Does that mean that standing in an alley means you are doing something illegal? No. Unfortunately, human beings often look to make associations that oversimplify or even completely pervert reality. Just because some individuals use the dark web inappropriately does not mean that this is how everyone uses it. Dark web providers, like Tor, actively campaign against using the platform for any illegal activity and many users are committed to self-policing against any obscene content or trade on the platform.

The United States government has consistently declined to criminalize the dark web.[10] Both using the dark web and hosting a relay are perfectly legal.[11] In fact, individual states have recently passed legislation to preserve these rights and ensure that public institutions like libraries and universities have the right to host relays (which is immensely beneficial, considering the high levels of bandwidth these institutions can provide).[12] The trend is not to criminalize the dark web, but rather to preserve it. You can follow the steps in chapter 5 to install and use the dark web for yourself right now with no fear of criminal repercussions (though, if you are at work, you should as always check with your employer first!).

MYTH 5: THE DARK WEB
WILL STEAL MY PERSONAL INFORMATION

Reality: Recent advertisements have suggested that your personal information may be stolen and sold on the dark web. We want to address two myths here: 1) that your information can be stolen while you are using the dark web, and 2) that your information is sold on the dark web.

Let's start with the first myth. No, your information cannot be stolen when you are on the dark web. That's the point of the dark web and of this whole book: increased privacy! Unless you willingly give somebody your information while using the dark web, they are not going to be able to retrieve it.

What about the second myth? This is what the commercials are always talking about: dark web auctions where your data is sold. Could it happen? Maybe. Does it happen as often as the advertisements claim? No. Advertisers are capitalizing on exactly what we discussed at the beginning of this chapter. People do not know what the dark web is, but it sounds creepy, and we have all read a story about evil things going on there. It seems reasonable that these auctions are happening. Having used the dark web ourselves and being familiar with its forums and sites, we have never run across a single one of these auctions. That does not mean that we have not heard of it happening, but it's incredibly uncommon.[13] Often when it happens, it is a large quantity of credit card numbers that were collected as part of some well-publicized breach. By the time they end up for sale, months or years will have passed. If you follow the news, you should have plenty of time to cancel your card before it gets to this point.

MYTH 6: I NEED TO BUY SOME SPECIAL HARDWARE OR SOFTWARE IN ORDER TO USE THE DARK WEB

Reality: All that is required to use the dark web is a free download of a browser platform.[14] Chapter 5 will discuss step by step how to download three of the most popular dark web platforms to your computer.

SOME PROMINENT REPORTS ON THE DARK WEB

Congressional Research Service Report

On March 10, 2017, the United States Congressional Research Service released a report on the dark web for the benefit of congressmen/women and the public.[15] The report generally has good information on the dark web (and we would expect nothing less from the CRS). Particularly, the report does a good job of discussing how the dark web, rather than being a massive pain for the United States government, can be a tremendous boon, preserving the anonymity of law enforcement for tip lines and investigations and protecting the military from hacks while tracking the behavior of potential terrorist groups.

The report, however, is somewhat misleading. For instance, we would argue that suggesting the dark web is closely related to the deep web is inappropriate. Deep web sites can be accessed via the regular Internet, given the right credentials. Generally, it is only a login or CAPTCHA box that hides these sites from Google's purview. The dark web, as we have discussed, requires a special browser to access. The report also neglects to mention the mainstream sites that now call Tor home, like the *New York Times* and Facebook. It is worth noting that the primary target of this report is legislators, which is why there is a section dedicated to government use of the platform.

Dark Web Scan Websites

Without naming any names (that seems like a risk not worth taking), we want to discuss some specific claims made by services that sell the idea of a "dark web scan." First, let's look briefly at the service itself. What does it do? It does not scan the dark web live. As the websites claim, they scan documents dating back over a decade. This is done by literally visiting sites and saving the data directly. It is not a live scan of current data existing on the dark web. This is something that a professor of information science and a few graduate students using the dark web archive (discussed in chapters 5 and 6) could realistically accomplish.

It is made to seem as though it is some state-of-the-art technology that breaks through the barriers of the dark web to identify whether your information is used. The major problem is that, when selling your information, the sellers do not provide your information publicly. They are not going to say, "For sale $100: John Doe's credit account with username dfiasdj2423 and password 234324hjlk." If they did that, then what would be the purpose of buying the information? It's already available right there. If and when such sales occur, the ads look more like this: "1000 Bank X account information: $10,000." Nothing in that posting identifies whether your information is being sold or not. These scans are not going to know whether your information is being sold (in the very unlikely case that it actually is). What these scans do, however, is provide for-profit companies with inordinate amounts of your personal information.

What about the articles these companies publish on news websites and blogs where they "explain" the dark web? It is worth noting that most of these articles discuss data breaches, not the dark web, and that they have few or no references (and those references they do have often link to other articles on the same website). There are also frequently disclaimers at the bottom of these articles that say something along the lines of "The opinions expressed in this article are the author's alone, and are not associated with any bank or company," which is suspicious considering that the author is generally an employee (or even executive) of these so-called dark web scan companies. These articles have even taken the infamous fake-news form of clickbait titles and advertising placement.

CONCLUSION

In this chapter, we wanted to dispute some common myths about the dark web and set the scene for the remaining chapters of this book. The most important thing to remember as you read is that this text is not meant to be a passive read, but rather an interactive guide. You are invited to follow along as we install a dark web browser, visit websites, and conduct research.

NOTES

1. Tor Project, "Tor: Overview," accessed October 22, 2018, https://www.torproject.org/about/overview.html.en.

2. Kelley Misata, "The Tor Project: An Inside View," *XRDS: Association for Computing Machinery* 20, no. 1 (Fall 2013), 45–47.

3. Andrew G. Fanno, "Multistakeholder Approach to Internet Governance: A Collaborative Effort Combating Illegal Internet Activities," *Suffolk Transnational Law Review* 38, no. 1 (Winter 2015): 69.

4. Fenwick McKelvey, "We Like Copies, Just Don't Let the Others Fool You: The Paradox of the Pirate Bay," *Television & New Media* 16, no. 8 (2015): 734–50.

5. Albert N. Greco, "The Kirtsaeng and SCI-HUB Cases: The Major US Copyright Cases in the Twenty-First Century," *Publishing Research Quarterly* 33, no. 3 (2017): 238–53.

6. Filipe N. Ribeiro, Koustuv Saha, Mahmoudreza Babaei, Lucas Henrique, Johnnatan Messias, Oana Goga, Fabricio Benevenuto, Krishna P. Gummadi, and Elissa M. Redmiles, "On Microtargeting Socially Divisive Ads: A Case Study of Russia-Linked Ad Campaigns on Facebook," paper presented at ACM Conference on Fairness, Accountability, and Transparency (Atlanta, GA, January 30, 2019), http://delivery.acm.org/10.1145/3290000/3287580/p140-Ribeiro.pdf.

7. Robert W. Gehl, *Weaving the Dark Web: Legitimacy on Freenet, Tor, and I2P* (Cambridge, MA: MIT Press, 2018).

8. United Nations Office on Drugs and Crime, *World Drug Report 2017*, https://www.unodc.org/wdr2017/field/WDR_2017_presentation_long.pdf.

9. Electronic Frontier Foundation, "Tor: Myths and Facts," September 10, 2015, https://www.eff.org/document/tor-myths-and-facts.

10. Alex Hern, "US Government Increases Funding for Tor, Giving $1.8m in 2013," *Guardian*, July 29, 2014, https://www.theguardian.com/technology/2014/jul/29/us-government-funding-tor-18m-onion-router.

11. Tor Project, "Tor: Overview."

12. Gareth Owen and Nick Savage, "The Tor Dark Net," Global Commission on Internet Governance Paper Series, no. 20 (September 2015), https://www.cigionline.org/sites/default/files/no20_0.pdf.

13. Sara Aniello and Stefano Caneppele, "Selling Stolen Goods on the Online Markets: An Exploratory Study," *Global Crime* 19, no. 1 (2018): 42–62.

14. Eric Jardine, "The Dark Web Dilemma: Tor, Anonymity, and Online Policing," Global Commission on Internet Governance Paper Series, no. 21 (September 2015), https://www.cigionline.org/sites/default/files/no.21.pdf.

15. Kristin Finklea, "Dark Web," United States Congressional Research Service 7-5700, July 7, 2015, https://archive.org/details/R44101DarkWeb-crs.

5

How to Access the Dark Web

The dark web is quite easy to access. Anyone with a basic knowledge of Internet downloads and the required administrative permissions on a computer can accomplish it. This chapter provides a step-by-step guide to installing three of the major dark web platforms—Tor, Freenet, and I2P—and offers advice to take during the download process to further enhance security and privacy.

A NOTE ON FIREWALLS AND DARK WEB DOWNLOADS

It is likely that the firewall on your computer will block features of the platform you download. Blocking these features will limit the full capabilities of the platform. Ultimately, you must decide whether to allow the firewall to block the features. The platforms should still work okay no matter which option you choose.

HOW TO INSTALL TOR

Tor is the most popular dark web software. This is largely due to its ease of use. Tor was designed with a typical Internet user in mind and this is evident throughout the user experience.[1] It is also the most versatile of the dark web platforms—available on Windows, Mac, and Linux devices. The following section will describe step by step how to install it on each device.

Installation Set-Up (complete no matter which type of device you use)

1. Using a standard web browser (like Firefox or Mozilla), navigate to the Tor website: www.torproject.org.
2. On the website's home page is a large button that reads "Download Tor." Click on this button.
3. You will be directed to another page that again prompts you to "Download Tor Browser." Click this button.
4. Tor's download defaults to the operating system you are currently using. For instance, if you are using Windows, it will default to a Windows download. If you would like, you can select another operating system by following the links just to the right of the download button.
5. Specify the download language using the drop-down menu just below the button (this defaults to English).

Complete Install on Windows

1. For Windows, select the "Download" button and allow the install file to download.
2. When the download is complete, double-click on the file that appears at the bottom of the screen. If this file does not appear, you may go to your file explorer (the folder at the bottom of the screen), click on "Desktop," and search for the download file by name.

3. You will again be prompted to select a language (this defaults to the language you specified earlier). This will set the language for the download as well as the browser once it has downloaded.
4. Select an install location. Typically the default location is fine unless you have a specific install location already in mind or created.
5. It will take a few moments for Tor to download once you select "Install." When this has completed you will be asked whether you would like to add shortcuts and run the browser. It is advisable that you keep both selected and hit "Finish."

Complete Install on Mac

1. Select "Download" and open the .dmg file.
2. Save the .dmg file to the Applications folder. This will create a desktop application for Tor as soon as the files have downloaded.
3. You will be prompted to select a language before proceeding with the install.

Complete Install on Linux

1. Select "Download" to retrieve a zipped file package.
2. To extract the files in the package, enter the command
   → Tar –xvJf (package name)
   Where (package name) should be the name of the file package you downloaded.
3. When the files have been extracted, enter
   → Cd tor-browser_(language)
   Where (language) should be the language of your download.
4. Select the browser icon.

Finalizing the Install

When Tor has installed you will be greeted by a "Connect to Tor" dialogue box. When you select "Connect," your computer will establish a connection to the Tor network, which may take a few minutes. You will have to repeat this process each time you open the Tor browser. When your browser has connected it will launch; you are ready to begin your dark web browsing session.

Tor on Android

Individuals who own an Android phone can download Tor for their device. In doing this it is important to select the correct application, as there are, unfortunately, many fraudulent applications that aim to deceive. The official Android version of Tor is Orbot. It is searchable in the Android/Google Play store. The app is very simple,

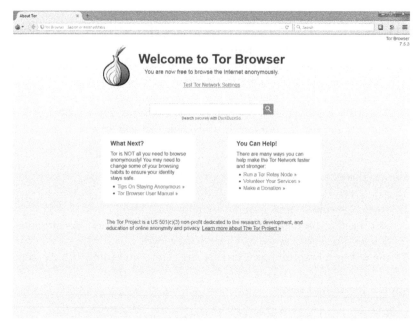

Figure 5.1.   Tor Browser Home Page

essentially providing the functionality to activate Tor while using your device and providing the option to add a virtual private network or bridge. That's it. There is no Tor browser as there is for the desktop, but DuckDuckGo privacy browser is highly recommended to serve this end. The combination of Orbot and DuckDuckGo will make it difficult for anyone to track you from your device.

Here are some simple tips to further improve your security while installing the Tor browser.

Do Not Edit Any Install Files. Tor is already configured to run as optimally as possible. Editing files may compromise the integrity of your download. Only do so if you truly know what you are doing!

Don't Attempt to Install Flash Player. While Flash remains a popular platform for games, videos, and other interactive elements, its security is horrendous. Enabling it is putting your data at risk.

HTTP vs. HTTPS. You may have noticed that the prefix for the web address in your search bar may read alternatively HTTP and HTTPS. HTTP stands for Hypertext Transfer Protocol. Consider it the "To:"

line on an email message; it tells the server that hosts a website that a user wants to access that site. In that sense, it is possible to acquire information about who is making the request. HTTPS—the *S* standing for "secure"—provides an extra layer of encryption that help prevent unauthorized access to your data. To maximize your security on Tor, the browser automatically defaults to use the HTTPS version of a site. There are, however, sites that are not compatible with HTTPS and these should be avoided if possible. The Tor browser includes a nifty browser plug-in called HTTPS Everywhere, provided by the Electronic Freedom Frontier (EFF). As you browse the dark web, it is constantly analyzing the sites you are accessing and does its best to access those using HTTPS.

HOW TO INSTALL FREENET

Freenet is far different from the other dark web platforms discussed in this chapter. Freenet is less dynamic than Tor. It is also more difficult to use. Its learning curve is steep. The platform, however, provides several advantages that will be discussed later in this chapter. Directions for installing Freenet are listed below.

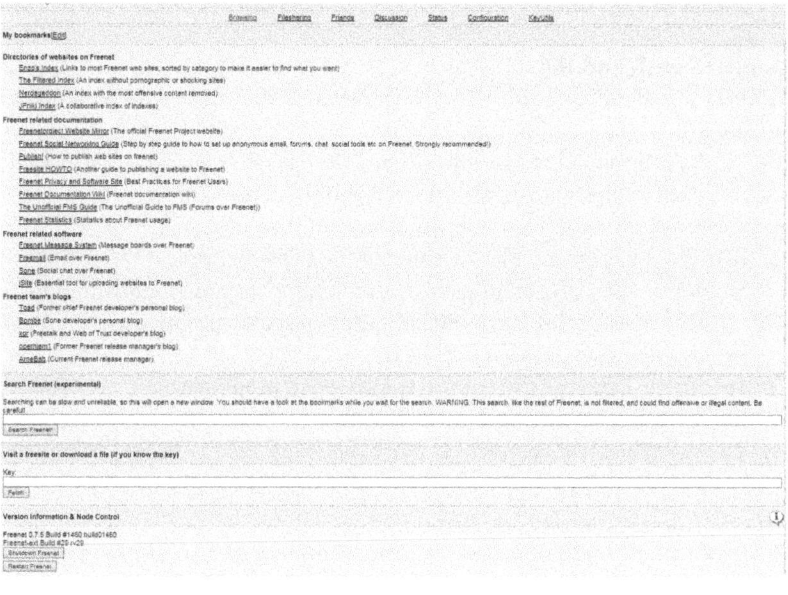

Figure 5.2. Freenet Home Page

Installation Set-Up

1. Navigate to the Freenet website: https://freenetproject.org/index.html.
2. At the top of the screen, select "Download" from the options bar.

Complete Install on Windows

1. Select the "Download Freenet" button.
2. Specify the language for your download when prompted.
3. Select a location to download the files (again, the default is likely fine).
4. Freenet will ask whether you would like to add a folder to the start menu. Adding this feature will improve the ease with which you can access the program after it downloads. On the next screen you will be able to add a desktop shortcut as well.
5. Review your selections and click "Install."
6. The download will complete in a few moments. Select "Finish" to proceed.

Complete Install on Mac

1. Select the "Download Freenet for OSX" button.
2. Specify the language for your download when prompted.
3. Review your selections and click "Install."
4. Add Freenet to your applications and begin the download.
5. The download will complete in a few moments. Select "Finish" to proceed.

Complete Install on Linux
The Linux install differs slightly from Windows and Mac. Since Freenet is created in Java, you will need a Java Runtime Environment for the software to run properly in Linux. This environment can be downloaded from http://www.java.com. When this install has been completed you can proceed with the Freenet install.

1. Retrieve the necessary files by entering the following code:
   → Wget 'https://github.com/freenet/fred/releases/download/build01480/new_installer_offline_1480.jar' -0new_installer_offline.jar;
   → Java –jar new_installer_offline.jar;
2. Specify the language for your download when prompted.
3. Review your selections and click "Install."
4. The download will complete in a few moments. Select "Finish" to proceed.

FREENET SECURITY OPTIONS

Each time you access Freenet you will be asked to select your security settings. The options to choose from are low security, high security, and custom. With the low-security setting you may access any of the content stored on a public Freenet, but this comes with a higher risk that your access could be compromised (as it is being distributed across a number of networks). With high-security access, you can only access sites of those specified as "friends." Finally, the custom option will allow you to tweak settings to meet your access and security desires. Each of these options is detailed below.

Low Security. For the high-access/low-security option, you will be redirected to select datastore size. Generally, a larger datastore is advised, though if you experience issues the size may need to be reduced. Next, indicate if you have any limits on your bandwidth (most likely, you will select "no"). You will then be asked to select your transfer rate (connection speed). Again, the larger the selection the better. At this point you will be transferred to the home page of Freenet.

High Security. For the limited-access/high-security option, you will first be reminded that you need to add friends in order to access content. You can add friends from the low security page or later on the "add friends" page that will appear after your connection is established. Next you will be asked to select your encryption level. Using a high level of encryption will necessitate a password, while maximum encryption will create a temporary encryption key that will clear all Freenet activity upon closing the browser. You will then create a node, which is an identifier that will distinguish you (in an otherwise anonymous environment) from other users when your friends connect. Then, as with the low-security selection, you will be asked to select a datastore size, bandwidth limits, and a transfer rate.

Custom Configuration. With a custom configuration, you will be able to update and add plug-ins to the program. You will next be asked several questions to determine the level of security and type of connection you require. Based on these responses Freenet will establish a connection and ask you to select datastore size, bandwidth limits, and transfer rate.

HOW TO INSTALL I2P

I2P, the Invisible Internet Project, is similar to Tor in its design and Freenet in its popularity. It is more difficult than Tor or Freenet to run, as it requires additional steps to be taken after installation in order to work effectively. I2P, however, benefits from being a lesser-used platform. This means increased security for users.[2] There is a bit of give-and-take with these platforms that give them their individual value. For I2P it just happens to be its lower popularity and higher security.

Installation Set-Up

1. Navigate to I2P's download site (https://geti2p.net/br/download) and select the file next to the logo for your operating system. This will begin the download.

Complete Install on Windows

1. When the file has downloaded, double-click on it.
2. Select your language from the options provided.
3. Choose an install location for the browser. As with the prior two platforms, the default install location is probably fine unless you have a specific location planned.
4. Select whether you would like to add shortcuts for the browser.
5. Click "Install."

Complete Install on Mac

1. Open a line terminal. To do this, open your Applications folder, then open your Utilities folder and select "Terminal."
2. Enter the following line of code:
   → Java –jar i2pinstall_(version).jar
   where (version) is the version number of the install.
3. When the file has downloaded, double-click on it.
4. Select your language from the options provided.
5. Select whether you would like to add shortcuts for the browser.
6. Click "Install."

Complete Install for Linux

1. Open a line terminal. To do this, open your Applications folder, then open your Utilities folder and select "Terminal."
2. Enter the following line of code:
   → Java –jar i2pinstall_(version).jar
   where (version) is the version number of the download
3. When the file has downloaded, double-click on it.
4. Select your language from the options provided.
5. Select whether you would like to add shortcuts for the browser.
6. Click "Install."

WHAT OTHER STEPS SHOULD
BE TAKEN TO IMPROVE SECURITY ON I2P?

To improve privacy for I2P you can adjust the bandwidth in your browser. To do this, find the "Configure Bandwidth" icon under the "Applications and Configurations" heading. By increasing your bandwidth settings you strengthen the capability of the full I2P network. Increasing the rates and percent share as high as possible while meeting the specifications of your computer is recommended. You may also protect the security on your physical computer by creating an authorization login for your I2P connection. To create an authorization, navigate to the I2CP tab at the top of the I2P client configuration screen (the same screen from which you adjust bandwidth settings). Click the box next to "Require username and password," and select the name and password of your choice. This will ensure that another user on the same computer will not be able to access your I2P data (these settings may also need to be configured within the host browser you are using).

Navigating the Router Console

When I2P downloads, you will be directed to the Router Console, which opens in your default Internet browser. This is what we would (endearingly!) call a confusing hodgepodge of buttons and displays. It is great for those who are experienced with I2P, but not so much for a novice user who is just trying to figure it out. Believe us, we know that this display can intimidate someone into just shutting down the program and not looking back. But fear not! We're here to provide some direction. In figure 5.3, we provide a notation on the function of every button on I2P's home screen. Consider this the roadmap to the router console.

As a first experience you can use email and browse eepsites (I2P's equivalent of Tor's onion sites, or of the mainstream Internet's websites) with relative ease. To access these features you will need to route your I2P connection through your web browser. To do this, follow these steps:

1. Go to the settings on your browser (you will likely find this on whatever browser you are using by locating a drop-down menu on the right side of the page and selecting "Settings" or "Internet options").
2. Navigate to the "Connections" tab and click on "Local Area Network Settings."
3. Click in the box underneath "Proxy Server" and enter as the address 127.0.0.1 and for the port 4444.
4. Select "OK."

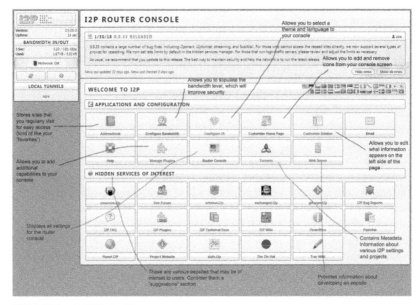

Figure 5.3.   I2P Home Page

You are now configured to use I2P. *Please note* that you will need to go back to this location and disable the proxy server before resuming normal Internet browsing. You can do this by following the directions above, then deleting the information under the proxy server.

To access the email service in I2P, follow these steps:

1. Find the email icon located near the middle of the first row of icons under the heading "Applications and Configurations." Click on this icon.
2. When the login screen loads, new users should select "Create account" on the bottom-right side of the login box.
3. On the "Create account" page, enter an account name, a password, and the name you would like to have displayed for your account. Click "Proceed."

You now have a secure email account on the I2P network. You can use this email to connect with other I2P users just as you would with a traditional email account.

All the buttons under "Hidden Services of Interest" will take you to an eepsite (you can check whether you are using an eepsite by looking for the .i2p suffix in your address bar). There are hundreds of eepsites available through I2P, many of which will be explored in chapters 6, 7, and 8 of this book.

SIMILARITIES AND DIFFERENCES BETWEEN PLATFORMS

All three platforms discussed in this chapter are anonymous (dark web) platforms. There are, however, several unique aspects of each platform that may appeal to certain users. Some of these differences have been mentioned throughout the chapter but will receive a more detailed treatment here.

Tor is the most utilized of any of the dark web platforms—so much so that the word *Tor* has become almost synonymous with the dark web.[3] It has substantial financial backing and benefits from years of research and testing. It boasts users from almost every nation across the globe. Tor also has more developers than its competitors, including mainstream organizations like Facebook. As far as sheer size and experience, it cannot be surpassed. Tor is also less susceptible to attacks and censorship at the national level. The size of the network buffers it from attempts to be shut down.

Freenet stores data in permanent repositories, meaning that your information can be safely stored forever.[4] Other platforms host forums that are temporary. As time passes access can become strained. Websites on Tor or I2P may also store data, but this data can be destroyed at the discretion of the site's owner. Freenet is more of a forum for peer-to-peer sharing rather than a platform for websites. While it is very good at what it does, what it does can be limited.

I2P incorporates elements from both Tor and Freenet. It has websites (eepsites) like Tor but is also conducive to peer-to-peer exchange like Freenet. It is generally faster than both of its rivals.[5] I2P also has fewer users than Tor and Freenet, which means that there are fewer individuals seeking to acquire your information through coercion (e.g., scamming you, trying to trick you into following an untrustworthy link).

Browsing Environment

The Tor browser may look familiar to some users. This is because the browser is actually created with a modified Mozilla Firefox browser. Firefox is an open-source software package with significant support built in, making it ideal for the adaptation (it also carries the benefit of allowing users to implement Firefox plug-ins, as discussed in chapter 6). The traditional Firefox package is modified by adding the Tor router features on the back end and automatically installing the HTTPS Everywhere extension (which provides a more secure connection to Internet sites).[6]

Because the Tor browser is housed within the Firefox shell, users can access World Wide Web sites in addition to dark web sites. These World Wide Web sites are not as secure, because the connection between the exit relay (the final server in the chain before connecting to the website) and the target site will be unencrypted, meaning that the exit relay and its Internet service provider can see what sites are being accessed, and potentially modify that access, even if they cannot see *who* is accessing it). This is an important note for educators to keep in mind while instructing others about Tor.

Freenet and I2P do not provide this same functionality. Freenet runs in your default browser, but only provides protection for Freenet sites. You can type in another site address and navigate to that site, but it will not be secured. I2P requires you to reconfigure your local area network, which prevents you from accessing World Wide Web sites.

THIRD-PARTY APPLICATIONS

There are several third-party applications that claim to incorporate a dark web network (usually Tor) into their service. These should be evaluated very carefully. Some of these apps are fraudulent and do not provide full protection. Others may even do the opposite of provide protection, preying on your trust to steal your data. The best idea is always to download the official application and the services available on it—but if that, for some reason, is not available, let's examine some of the more popular and trustworthy third-party apps.

Vuze. Vuze is a BitTorrent (secure peer-to-peer file sharing network) service that provides functionality in both Tor and I2P. While Vuze has been criticized for implementing involuntary adware in its install,[7] it is generally considered secure. The service has been criticized by some for using an exorbitantly large amount of bandwidth. For those interested in using peer-to-peer file sharing, Freenet or I2P's built-in services may be better suited.

BitMessage. BitMessage is a platform to send encrypted messages, developed and refined to be resistant to warrantless government surveillance. BitMessage can be run from within Tor and I2P, or external to these networks. The platform is well received, though there are many similar platforms available across the dark web.

What about Tor for iPhone? There are no official Tor applications for the iPhone, though there are many apps that claim to offer this service. In fact, some of these applications contain spyware and malware that will damage your phone and your privacy. The most widely publicized example of this was the Tor Browser Bundle, an unauthorized application released in 2014. This application damaged many phones by introducing malware that the phones could not counteract.

CHOOSING WHICH PLATFORM TO USE

This chapter presents information on how to install three different dark web platforms—but which one is the right one for you or your organization? If you are looking for the "mainstream" dark web, you will undoubtedly want to go with the Tor browser. Want a platform that has similar functionality to Tor but is less mainstream? I2P may be the perfect fit. Just want to distribute files to friends without the concern of surveillance? Freenet could be the ideal choice. Any platform may be acceptable for your need as an individual. Certain platforms may work better than others for organizations as a whole. The platform that will best suit you ultimately depends on your specific needs. The following sections will explore the suitability of each platform for given conditions, to help guide your decision.

I Am a Dark Web Novice Who Just Wants to See What It Is All About

If you are just looking for a learning experience, Tor is likely the best choice. Tor is used by millions of people each month.[8] It is easy to download and reasonably easy to use. Tor can be used to access such major sites as Facebook and ProPublica, in addition to the "hidden sites." The word *Tor* in fact has become interchangeable with the term *dark web* (it's like the Kleenex of the tissue industry). It is frequently the subject of research and news reporting. For educational exposure to the dark web, you really cannot go wrong with Tor.

You may, however, find both I2P and Freenet to be compelling as well. Both platforms are very different from Tor and thus provide unique experiences. While they may be slightly more difficult to download and use, they provide a different, and more complete look at the various dark web platforms and peer-to-peer file-sharing networks.

I Am Looking to Avoid Government Surveillance and Private Companies Selling My Data

Any of the dark web platforms are a tremendous upgrade over the mainstream web browsers. The one that is right for you will depend on your specific needs. Tor is the most popular, but this also means that more people are on there looking for ways to trick you into voluntarily revealing your personal information. I2P is similar to Tor but less popular, which means both fewer options for web browsing and fewer individuals trying to coerce information out of you. Freenet is secure but has fewer capabilities than either of the other two platforms. Try out all of them and see which works best for your needs!

I Am Looking for a Secure Platform to Communicate with Friends and Family

Freenet is likely the best platform for you. Freenet provides an optimal, ultrasecure platform for sharing files between groups of friends. While both Tor and I2P have forums for file sharing, Freenet cuts through the websites to point you directly to a peer-to-peer file sharing platform.

I Live in a Country Where Censorship Bars Access to Certain Information

Any of the dark web platforms may work for you, but you may need to find a different way to download the platform. Most countries that employ censorship block access to the home sites of Tor, I2P, and Freenet.[9] Fortunately, there are some other options to connect. The main method is through the utilization of a mirror (essentially the same data on the official website posted elsewhere to outrace censors). The most popular site for accessing mirrors is GitHub (https://github.com). Tor also lists many of its mirrors at https://www.torproject.org/getinvolved/mirrors.html.en. Information about mirrors may also be shared covertly in high-censorship countries through legal communication forums online and in person.

Another resource that may enable you to access information about the dark web and where to download it is the Internet Archive. For those who are not familiar with the Internet Archive, it is a website—accessible at https://web.archive.org—that catalogs website "histories" or "captures." These captures are copies of a website as it appeared at a given point in time, often dating back to the late 1990s. Tor's Internet archive dates back to 2007 and contains thousands of captures, with new captures added daily.

I Am Looking for a Platform to Download on All the Computers in My Organization/Library

The platform that will work best for your organization depends on its particular needs. Freenet would be ideal for organizational file sharing for small organizations. Certainly, compared to Google Drive, SharePoint, and Dropbox, Freenet excels in security while retaining the capacity to quickly and easily share large quantities of files. For use in research and industry, Tor and I2P will better suit your needs. As with any technology decision, you will want to consider what your user looks like in making a decision. Keep in mind that Tor is the most widely utilized platform and will likely appeal most to a general population.

For a library or information organization, the best platform will depend on the size and composition of your user base and what rights/types of access you want your users to have. In most library and information organizations, Tor will work well for your needs. It was designed to be user friendly and is similar to the traditional Internet Explorer in regard to layout and navigation. It *feels* like an Internet browser. It comes with a user manual and a search guide, both listed right on the home page. It is also the easiest to install and thus may be more time effective for the commitment of library staff.

Freenet may provide certain features that would be useful to library patrons beyond what Tor provides. The secure file sharing offered by the site presents a way for patrons to store and disseminate their work without the risk of data theft or loss. All the platforms are free to install, so the major factors to consider are time commitment and suitability for your audience.

IS INSTALLING A DARK WEB
PLATFORM ON OUR LIBRARY'S COMPUTERS LEGAL?

Yes, it is legal and is a great way to fulfill the missions of our libraries! In fact, we recently conducted a qualitative comparison of the benefits of the dark web according to the Tor Project information page and the American Library Association's (ALA) mission, vision, and values. We found that the dark web aligns directly with three of the ALA's four strategic directives (advocacy; information policy; and equity, diversity, and inclusion), seven of its nine core value statements (extending and expanding library services in America and around the world; all types of libraries; all librarians working together; an open, inclusive, and collaborative environment; innovating; intellectual freedom; social responsibility),[10] and five of its eight key action areas (advocacy, diversity, equitable access, intellectual freedom, transforming libraries).[11]

It is important to note that there are some challenges with implementing the dark web in your library. Not all people will be supportive of this technology being available to the public, including possibly local, state, and federal governments. While this would hopefully not deter a library that is committed to providing privacy services to its patrons, it is certainly understandable why this would cause concern. This and many other legal and ethical concerns will be covered in detail in chapter 7.

SHOULD I ALLOW MY CHILD
TO DOWNLOAD A DARK WEB PLATFORM?

Every parent must decide for him/herself whether to allow a child to download and use a dark web platform. You should realize that, as a component of the security features, most dark web platforms do not store browsing history locally. Unlike a traditional Internet browser, there is no search or browser history to be found. On the other hand, there are far fewer security issues with the dark web, so navigating to the wrong site does not necessarily put all your personal information at risk.

The authors of *Advances in Cyber Security* point out the risks of traditional Internet browsing:

> You've told your kids they shouldn't share personally identifying information online, but they may be sharing their location simply by not concealing their IP address. Increasingly, IP addresses can be literally mapped to a city or even street location and can reveal other information about how you are connecting to the Internet. In the United States, the government is pushing to make this mapping increasingly precise.[12]

Both the dark web and the Internet carry concerns as to the content young users may be able to access; the dark web, however, has more content that could be deemed illegal. One point in Tor's favor is that sites with mature or illegal content are not publicly advertised or readily accessible via a search engine and thus children can use the platform just as they would any Internet browser without fear of accidental exposure. A child likely won't know any different and the parents can ensure greater security for both the child and their personal information.

CONCLUSION

This chapter details the process of selecting and downloading the anonymous browser of your choice. While the download process itself is not particularly difficult, deciding what browser is best for your purpose and what to do once you have successfully downloaded it can be a challenge. This guide hopefully addresses those concerns and holds your hand, so to speak, in downloading and exploring the basic facets of the three major dark web browsers. In subsequent chapters we will explore what you can do with these browsers now that they are downloaded and address legal and ethical concerns associated with personal and organizational use of the dark web.

NOTES

1. The Tor Project, "Relay Users," accessed June 8, 2018, https://metrics.torproject.org/userstats-relay-country.html.

2. I2P Project, "I2P Compared to Tor," November 1, 2016, https://geti2p.net/en/comparison/tor.

3. Eric Jardine, "The Dark Web Dilemma: Tor, Anonymity, and Online Policing," Global Commission on Internet Governance Paper Series, no. 21 (September 2015), https://www.cigionline.org/sites/default/files/no.21.pdf.

4. Ian Clarke, Scott G. Miller, Theodore W. Hong, Oskar Sandberg, and Brandon Wiley, "Protecting Free Expression Online with Freenet," *IEEE Internet Computing* 6, no. 1 (2002): 40–49.

5. I2P Project, "Comparing I2P to Other Projects," accessed March 3, 2018, www.i2pproject.net/en/comparison.

6. The Tor Project, "Normal People Use Tor," February 14, 2018, https://www.torproject.org/about/torusers.html.en.

7. Tomas Meskauskas, "Vuze Toolbar – how to remove browser redirects to search.conduit.com?," accessed March 27, 2019, https://www.pcrisk.com/removal-guides/6852-remove-vuze-toolbar-redirects.

8. The Tor Project, "Relay Users."

9. The Tor Project, "Top 10 Countries by Possible Censorship Events," accessed July 14, 2018, https://metrics.torproject.org/userstats-censorship-events.html.

10. American Library Association, "ALA's Core Values, Key Action Areas and Strategic Directions," accessed June 19, 2018, http://www.ala.org/aboutala/.

11. American Library Association, "Mission and Priorities," accessed March 21, 2018, www.ala.org/aboutala/node/229/.

12. Frank Hsu and Dorothy Marinucci, eds., *Advances in Cyber Security: Technology, Operations, and Experiences* (New York: Fordham University Press, 2013), 113–14.

6

How to Browse Using the Dark Web

Each dark web platform presents its own unique browsing methods. Some of these are more intuitive than others. The "browsing schematics" of each of the three major dark web platforms will be explored in the first section of this chapter. A major barrier for many users of the dark web is knowing how to access websites and what content/services these sites offer. The second half of this chapter will provide information about major dark web sites, including details on how to access the sites and what content they contain.

HOW TO BROWSE TOR

While Tor appears to be similar to Internet Explorer or Google Chrome, it is lacking one major feature: a proper search engine. Though it appears that a search engine is included on the home screen of Tor, this DuckDuckGo search only catalogs World Wide Web sites, not dark web sites. Dark web sites cannot be cataloged by a search engine. This is what gives the dark web its name.

WHY DO SEARCH ENGINES NOT WORK ON THE DARK WEB?

Search engines like Google and Bing rely on web crawlers to acquire information about sites. Web crawlers are pieces of computer code that are directed to navigate the web, following any links on web pages, and create a catalog or database of any information on these sites. Data from the sites are stored together (e.g., site title, address, key content). This is why you can search for "news" and still have CNN appear in the search. Web crawlers spread outward like . . . well, a web, automatically following links on pages and digging ever deeper into the sites. Web crawlers, however, cannot penetrate layers of encryption. As deep and dark web sites are encrypted, they cannot be accessed (this is, in fact, what gives the deep web that name—sites there are deeper than the web crawler can reach).

What the lack of search engines means for users is that they will simply have to know the sites they want to visit. In the twenty-first century some users may fail to realize just how often they rely on search engines. Fortunately, the second half of this chapter functions as a proto-encyclopedia of the dark web, where major sites will be listed for perusal.

In terms of actually navigating to sites on Tor, it is no different than entering a website address in a traditional web browser. The challenge is knowing what to enter, not how to enter it. One option that can help emulate a natural discovery experience (in addition to this book) is referring to the Hidden Wiki (https://thehiddenwiki. org/), a website that indexes many of the most popular Tor sites.

HOW TO BROWSE FREENET

Unlike Tor, Freenet does not look like a traditional web browser—even though it opens right within your default browser. Rather, it presents you with a web of links with brief explanations of what they represent. While a search is available at the bottom of the home screen, a quick test search will reveal just how little you can rely on it. Very little of the total information on the platform is indexed, and what does appear is not presented in a user-friendly format. The home screen also presents a list of links that may be of interest to the user. Several of these are described in part two of this chapter.

One observation you may make very early in your Freenet browsing experience is that the sites look simple—like something from the early days of the Internet. This is because Freenet sites are coded in HTML only, as a measure to reduce load times. HTML is a basic coding language that does not allow for dynamic and interactive features, only plain text, videos, and images. This has led to what some Freenet users call the 1990s time-machine effect.

Additionally, at the top of the screen are options for file sharing, friends, discussion, status, configuration, and keyutils. If you recall from chapter 5, the primary benefit of Freenet is secure peer-to-peer file sharing. It is through the links at the top of the page that this feature can be accessed. To quickly and securely share files, you may add individuals under the "Friends" section. Within the "Friends" tab you will be able to enter users' "node reference" to add them as friends. Your node reference is listed at the very bottom of the "Friends" page. After you enter a user's node reference you will have the opportunity to select the level of trust you have with the user and whether you want your other friends to be able to see this friend.

Once you have added a friend, you can view their Freenet site and direct file share. File sharing is done through the "File sharing" tab. You can select "Upload a file" from the drop-down menu to add content, which will be assigned an identifying key. When you want to download a file, you can access the corresponding tab from the drop-down menu and enter the identifying key to download content.

HOW TO BROWSE I2P

The first step in web browsing with I2P is to make sure the service is connected through your web browser. If the browser is not connected, refer to the previous chapter on how to install I2P.

RECONNECT TO I2P
SERVER DURING SUBSEQUENT VISITS

While users can still connect to the I2P server by following the method described in chapter 5 step by step, most web browsers will provide a shortcut to use during subsequent visits. To use this shortcut, simply open the settings on your browser and navigate to the "Connections" tab. Within "Connections," select "LAN settings." Finally, just click the box next to the port settings and hit enter. You're ready to go!

Remember, when you want to disconnect you need to go back and deselect this box— otherwise you won't be able to access surface web sites!

As discussed in chapter 5, I2P presents a medium between the familiar feel of Tor and the secure, file sharing capabilities of Freenet. As with the Tor browser, I2P's eepsites can be accessed by entering an address directly into the address bar at the top of the screen. If you want a more natural browsing experience, then read on below.

The section of the I2P router console entitled "Hidden services of interest" could be seen as an index of popular I2P sites. We will explore each of these sites in part two of this chapter.

There are two items under "Applications and configurations" that may be of interest. The first is "Customize home page." Within this selection you can choose "home page," where you can select which applications you want to include on your home screen—which could be particularly useful for hiding certain content from immature users. You can also adjust the bandwidth, which can speed up the loading process. Finally, under "Peers" you can add or remove users who can see you and whom users on your browser (including you and other people who have access to your computer) can see.

The second item is "plug-ins," which can be accessed either through the "Customize home page" tab or by selecting the app on the router console. Within the plug-in app you can enter I2P plug-in URLs to install. Plug-ins will give you extra functionality on I2P. Some popular plug-ins will be listed in the second part of this chapter.

BRIEF HISTORY OF DARK WEB SITES

The dark web has been in existence in some form since the mid-1990s and thus so have dark web sites.[1] Long before the days of the well-known Silk Roads and Facebooks, there were simple file and communication exchanges among groups of authorized users. The earliest "dark web sites" were simple communication channels for US government operatives and global political dissidents to share information and coordinate endeavors.[2] This was the primary composition of the dark web networks for over a half decade.

True development of the dark web outside of government-led initiatives took place in 2000–2003 with the inception of Freenet and I2P. Most of the initial publications on these platforms were predicated on file sharing and communication exchanges. Websites were mostly blogs and may be compared to the early Myspace social network.

What could be called the start of the modern era for the dark web was the launch of "Tor: The Second-Generation Onion Router" in 2004.[3] This was the start of a sizeable public presence on the platform as well as the broad adoption of Tor's acronym. Some of the earliest dark web sites were those affiliated with the platforms' developers, such as the archives (http://yjuwkcxlgo7f7obs.onion) and the newsletter (http://kzcx36ytbsm5iogs.onion), but the website offerings grew quickly from there.

Finally, in 2014 Facebook became the first globally known World Wide Web site to launch a dark website. Two years later, ProPublica became the first major news site to launch a dark web version. These two sites led a flood of new, legitimate sites into the dark web networks. While the deep web comprises millions of websites, this recent spark in dark web popularity has been just enough to raise the number of dark web sites to more than one hundred thousand.[4]

MAJOR DARK WEB SITES

This section will provide information on dark web sites that may be of interest to you or your users. This is certainly not an exhaustive list. Rather, these are simply the major points of interest. Most of the sites discussed in this section are perfectly legal for anyone to visit. A few of the sites (listed in a separate section at the end of the Tor section) contain potentially immoral or illegal material and are included for reference *only*.

Sites on Tor

Available on Traditional Web

This list of dark web sites will start off with sites that are also available on the traditional web. Accessing these resources through the dark web provides the important benefit of security and privacy.

The *New York Times*
nytimes3xbfgragh.onion/
Launched in May 2018, the *New York Times* dark web site is a recent but significant contribution to the pantheon of Tor sites. Using the *New York Times* service, users can access the same articles published in the physical paper or on the World Wide Web site. Tor provides access to these materials even in high-censorship countries like China. Certain features such as logins to save articles may be disabled on the site.

ProPublica
propub3r6espa33w.onion/
ProPublica's dark web site was launched in early 2016 and received international attention for its efforts to provide global access to its resources. The major investigative news journal states that an investigation of censorship in China was a major factor in its creation of a dark web site.[5] Like the *New York Times*, ProPublica provides access to the same content on its dark web site that is available on its World Wide Web site. The dark site simply provides access to more users across the globe.

Facebook
facebookcorewwwi.onion/
Facebook's Tor site launched in 2014 and quickly became one of the most popular websites on Tor, with over a million monthly users.[6] Facebook's dark web site is an

attempt to provide access and privacy on its service for those who live within high-censorship countries. Users can log in to the dark web version of Facebook using the same credentials as on the World Wide Web version. Once logged in, users will see the same feed and have the same functionality as on the mainstream site. The service, it is important to note, does not necessarily protect your information from Facebook itself, but does protect it from third parties that might wish to take your data.

WikiLeaks
Wlupld3ptjvsgwqw.onion/
WikiLeaks's Tor service launched in 2015 for two reasons: first, to provide access to its data across the globe; and second, to allow a secure means for individuals to provide documents to the service. While WikiLeaks has a World Wide Web site, its dark web site has become popular, particularly in light of crackdowns on the site and its founder, Julian Assange.

not Evil
hss3vro2hsxfogfq.onion/
not Evil was established in 2015, after previously being known by the name of TorSearch, which itself was available on Tor since at least 2008. It is definitely not Google, but not Evil does attempt to archive as many dark web pages as possible on its site. Most searches will not get you to what you're looking for, but if a user just has no idea where to go, then not Evil is a place to start.

Academic Sites and Journals

Sci-Hub
scihub22266oqcxt.onion/
Sci-Hub was established by Alexandra Elbakyan in 2011, purportedly in response to the arrest and prosecution of famed Internet activist Aaron Swartz.[7] Sci-Hub was developed to provide free access to millions of academic papers that would otherwise be held behind a paywall. Sci-Hub is a highly criticized platform, with many journal publishers claiming copyright infringement. Sci-Hub's World Wide Web site was shut down in 2015, but several versions exist today, including on the dark web. Note: It infringes on copyright law of the United States to upload copyrighted papers to Sci-Hub without the express permission of the copyright holder.

American Journal of Freestanding Research Psychology
http://qtsdq6tkszhxost2.onion/
The *American Journal of Freestanding Research Psychology* was launched in 2018 with the objective to relieve pressure on researchers who might wish to publish works that would be unpopular in their home country. This academic journal is published free and online on the dark web. It accepts submissions for the topic of research psychology.

Other Legal Sites

Freedom of the Press Foundation

freepress3xxs3hk.onion/

The Freedom of the Press Foundation opened its dark web site in 2013 as a means for individuals to submit news stories anonymously. The objectives of the organization are to raise funds to support organizations that fight censorship and to disseminate news that might be objectionable in certain countries. Among the foundation's well-known associates are Chelsea Manning, Edward Snowden (the organization's president since 2016), and the Electronic Frontier Foundation.

Archive.is

archivecaslytosk.onion/

Not as extensive in its catalog as the Internet Archive, archive.is still provides many screen captures of various websites dating back to 2012. This site provides access to archived versions of sites that might otherwise be banned in some countries. Access to the World Wide Web version of this site has been blocked in several countries. This led to the organization creating the dark web version of its site.

Tor Broker

torbrokerge7zxgq.onion

Tor Broker was established in 2012 in the wake of the cryptocurrency boom. It is an expansive marketplace for cryptocurrency, especially Bitcoin. In addition to purchasing cryptocurrency, the site also allows users to use that currency to purchase stocks on several global markets. The service has been viewed critically by several governments and has been the victim of attempted shutdowns. The site, however, remains a major exchange for several popular cryptocurrencies.

Beneath VT

74ypjqjwf6oejmax.onion

Abandoned/prohibited area exploration has become a popular phenomenon in the new media of YouTube and Instagram. One of the more detailed and well-done explorations is documented on Tor. The Beneath VT project captures images and narratives from those who have traveled the steam tunnels that underlie the campus of Virginia Tech University. The site was first published on the dark web in 2012. The posts are well written and have received much international recognition.[8]

Onion Forum 2.0

2gxxzwnj52jutais.onion

Onion Forum is a discussion forum for all things Tor. From troubleshooting to chatting and debate, the forum has a little to entice anyone. Onion Forum 2.0 launched in 2013 after the closing of the original Onion Forum, which itself was one of the first dark web sites to launch in the middle of the first decade of the 2000s.

Illegal Sites

Silk Road

silkroad7rn2puhj.onion/ (defunct)

This site is largely responsible for giving the dark web the bad name it has today. Silk Road was launched in early 2011 by Ross William Ulbricht (known online by the pseudonym Dread Pirate Roberts). The site served as a marketplace for all things illegal. At its height, Silk Road brought in about $500 million per year and sold thousands of illegal goods and services from its site.[9] The biggest product for the site was drugs—primarily marijuana and cocaine—with weapons, pornography, and stolen data representing much smaller proportions.

DID SILK ROAD PERMANENTLY TARNISH THE DARK WEB?

The dark web was relatively unknown in popular culture until the mid-2010s. The singular event that launched the dark web into the mainstream was Operation Onymous. Though few know it by this name, the highly publicized shutdown of Silk Road and affiliated sites by the FBI is widely attributed as the cause for the dark web's notoriety. Many dark web supporters claim that, while the shutdown may have been necessary, the FBI did it in the most publicly visible way possible to permanently tarnish the reputation of the dark web. They couldn't shut down the platform, because of its admitted benefits but wanted to scare the average user away from exploring the platform. If this accusation is true (and even if it is not), was it successful?

In the three years following the Silk Road crackdown, there was very little positive publicity about the dark web, as the negative continued to seep into the mainstream as a plot point in TV dramas and a favorite of sensationalist news commentators. However, starting around the year 2016, the message began to turn in some circles. While there is still a large population that fixates on the negative aspects of the dark web, an increasingly large group has shown support for the platform through renewed advocacy efforts. More widely known surface web sites have joined the fold, and the userbase has grown and diversified. Though progress had stalled for a few years, it is now turning in a positive direction.

Silk Road was shut down in 2013 after the FBI tracked down Ross Ulbricht using his personal email address, contained in a post he had made in an Internet forum while creating the site.[10] Less than a month after Ulbricht's arrest, Silk Road 2.0 was opened. This version of the site was shut down in 2014 after its founders were uncovered. Most individuals who sold items on Silk Road were never identified. Issues with illegal activities on the dark web and the Silk Road case will be explored in more detail in chapter 7.

The Pirate Bay
/uj3wazyk5u4hnvtk.onion/
The Pirate Bay was founded in 2003 and was hosted on the World Wide Web for the first several years of its existence. Following the arrests of the site's founders in 2009 and bans on the site by several countries, the Pirate Bay founded its dark web site.[11] While not all content on the Pirate Bay is illegal, the site provides a platform for the exchange of copyrighted material and thus has been highly scrutinized by governments and content producers. Though the Pirate Bay is available on the regular Internet, this site is frequently victim to censorship tactics, particularly in the United States, Europe, the Middle East, China, India, and Australia. Thus the Pirate Bay's dark web site has become a more widely used version for individuals in these locations.

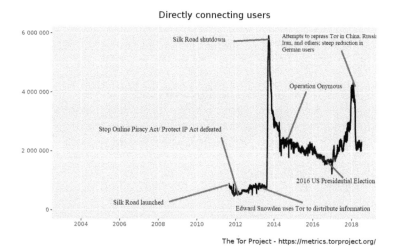

Figure 6.1.   Number of Users Connecting to Tor Network

Some Tor Plug-ins

Tor plug-ins can be accessed by clicking on the three horizontal lines to the right of the address bar and then selecting "add-ons" from the list that appears. There is no list of plug-ins, so you will have to search for them in the box provided.

Flash Player
There are many Flash Player downloads available for Tor. However, it is important
to remember—as mentioned in chapter 5—that flash players are notoriously bad at
securing your privacy. Install Flash Player at your own risk.

S3.Translator
This plug-in provides the translation capability of Google Translate on the Tor
browser. When it is enabled, you can simply highlight a portion of text, click the
S3 icon at the top of the screen, and receive a quick and accurate translation. The
plug-in was first offered in 2009 and has since been refined to improve translation
accuracy.

Email Extractor
Email Extractor has been made available since 2017. The plug-in automatically collects and compiles a list of all email addresses on sites that you visit. It is valuable
for research purposes.

QuickWiki
Want to know about something quickly without having to open a new browser with
Wikipedia? The QuickWiki plug-in pulls up a window on the browser where users
can easily look up information during the browsing experience. QuickWiki was
developed and released in 2017.

Western Illinois University Libraries Research Panel
This plug-in was developed for Firefox but runs on Tor as well. It is the first library-
based dark web tool that is compatible with the Tor browser. You can use this tool to
search a variety of databases for information while browsing the web.

Sites on Freenet

Indexes

Enzo's Index
http://localhost:8888/USK@XJZAi25dd5y7lrxE3cHMmM-xZ-c-hlPpK
LYeLC0YG5I,8XTbR1bd9RBXlX6j-OZNednsJ8Cl6EAeBBebC3jtMFU,AQAC
AAE/index/711/

Filtered Index
http://localhost:8888/USK@ozMQYaCEXnlHQQggITYSIeNSxqdMknqjOIYyC
dMKqJA,gJyID9FRxaM5zDql3D8-wHACAusOYa5Aag3M4tSEt~g,AQACAAE/
Index/726/
There are two major Freenet indexes that contain a listing of popular sites on the
platform: Enzo's Index and the Filtered Index. Enzo's Index is the most expansive
index on Freenet, containing thousands of entries. However, it includes links to sites

whose contents may be considered offensive. The Filtered Index is less expansive than Enzo's but has no potentially offensive content. Both indexes can be good places to start a browsing experience, but do not expect either to be similar to the ease of a Google search. The sites in the index often have peculiar titles that don't indicate the content, and the descriptions—if present at all—are often lacking.

Enzo's Index was the first major Freenet index, established in 2015. The Filtered Index was developed on a similar timeline to Enzo's Index and was also launched in 2015.

Flogs

By far the most common and popular element of Freenet is Freenet Blogs (referred to as flogs). Flogs have, in fact, existed from the very start of Freenet.[12] These uncensored outlets of expression may drum up imagery of an early Myspace clone. Of course, the great benefit of these flogs is anonymity that encourages true expression. This leads to flogs like those listed below, from individuals who might otherwise not feel comfortable expressing themselves. The moderators of the flogs have the ability to block users who post illegal content, ensuring the utility of the platform.

Toad's Flog
http://localhost:8888/USK@yGvITGZzrY1vUZK-4AaYLgcjZ7ysRqNTMfd-cO8gS-LY,-ab5bJVD3Lp-LXEQqBAhJpMKrKJ19RnNaZMIkusU79s,AQACAAE/toad/56/
Flog written by one of the creators of the Freenet platform.

A Girl Encrypted
http://localhost:8888/freenet:SSK@1wkOOF0iGlJf1Sc0nlfL2feDbl-6pvxMUJq1
MVXtjNA,vnyzCkUcG5J59N9xmL6632rggGtYjYOpl-2KfRhy5QQ,AQACAAE/agirlencrypted-0/
Blog from transgender woman during her transition

The Bomb in the Brain: The True Roots of Human Violence
http://localhost:8888/freenet:USK@GdLZYUATTsTESNHkbXKA7N4QCDK5v
aBXmtctppusZX8,CgInSQ6G6BzslEy-1l-3sVmD3abbMaqkY33r-qiXl1A,AQAC
AAE/BiB/3/
Blog about the effects of child abuse

Other Miscellaneous Freenet Sites and Services
Freenet News
http://localhost:8888/freenet:SSK@oNKbqlzD2v9yWmibEbjZHkT03HFAe4NjO
SaQdrunqb0,r-PDnTKzzGEU-YmvijHygVkMIM85MXCBzRBWfvzI5sY,AQAC
AAE/FreenetNews-6/

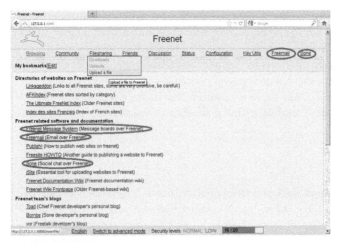

Figure 6.2.   Major Areas of Interest on Freenet

Freenet News was established in 2016 to provide information to the public. It is a primary spot for receiving updates on the platform and the world of the anonymous web.

Freenet Message System
http://localhost:8888/USK@0npnMrqZNKRCRoGojZV93UNHCMN-6UU
3rRSAmP6jNLE,-BG-edFtdCC1cSH4O3BWdeIYa8Sw5DfyrSV-TKdO5
ec,AQACAAE/fms/148/
The Freenet Message System has existed since the early days of the platform. It is a message board system for Freenet. You will need to install a download file to use this system. The download file is available from the "Message System" tab.

Freemail
Freemail is a plug-in that enables email messaging over the secure platform. It was a major early development to improve functionality on the platform. To install the plug-in, navigate to the Freenet home page. From there:

1. Hover over "Configurations" and from the drop-down list select "Plug-ins."
2. Under "Add an official plug-in," find the section entitled "Communication plugins."
3. Select the button next to the "weboftrust" plug-in and select "Load."
4. You will be returned to the same plug.in screen, where you should select the button next to "Freemail" and select "Load" again.
5. A "Freemail" tab will appear on the banner at the top of the screen. If it does not, repeat steps 1–4.

6. If you have not already created a community login, do so by hovering over "Community" on the top banner and then selecting "Log in."
7. Under "New identity," select "You can create a new identity here."
8. Select "Generate a new key" and click "Continue."
9. Enter a name and select "Continue."
10. Select "Continue" a final time; your login has been created.
11. Now, hover over Freemail and select "Log in."
12. Click on "You can add another account here."
13. Select your identity and add a password; select "Add account."
14. Your Freemail account has been established! You can now send and receive secure emails through Freenet.

Sone Social Network

Like Freenet, Sone Social Chat is a plug-in that can be added to the platform. Sone was an early development on Freenet that provides many of the same functionalities as I2P. To add Sone:

1. Hover over "Configuration" and select "Plug-ins."
2. Scroll down to "Add an unofficial plug-in;" in the "Plug-in URL" box, enter USK@nwa8lHa271k2QvJ8aa0Ov7IHAV-DFOCFgmDt3X6BpCI,Du QSUZiI~agF8c-6tjsFFGuZ8eICrzWCILB60nT8KKo,AQACAAE/sone/78/ sone-current.jar.
3. Select "Load."
4. When the plugin has loaded, a "Sone" tab will appear on the top ribbon. Hover over this tab and select "Log in" from the drop-down menu.
5. If you have already created a login (as described in the Freemail install guide), select this login and select "Continue."
6. You are now able to create and view messages in the system using the appropriate options under the "Sone" tab.

Sites on I2P

Like Freenet, I2P lacks "mainstream" sites. Rather, all eepsites are designed specifically for I2P users. The following is a list of just a few of these sites for your perusal. Remember that several of the more compelling and useful sites are listed at the bottom of the router console as displayed on the map in the previous chapter.

Eye Search

http://Eye.i2p

Eye Search, a longtime feature of the I2P platform, is its major search engine. This search engine—while not comprehensive—provides access to several eepsites that are not indexed elsewhere.

Library Genesis
http://p4swjett52gpafbbdkxwktfcwqzlo44k2ve6tzduhmmc2hbvj6nq.b32.i2p
Library Genesis (LibGen) was founded in 2011 as a free repository of scholarly articles and books, in the same vein as Sci-Hub (discussed in the section of Tor sites). These are materials that would normally be saved behind a paywall. LibGen was wrapped into the same 2015 case as Sci-Hub, which resulted in its .org site being shut down.[13] The site has since migrated to I2P, where it now holds over two million items. As with Sci-Hub, the content on LibGen infringes on copyright law in the United States.

Open Music
http://openmusic.i2p
This site streams free music hosted by various I2P users. Most of the music played on the platform is original music or copyright free.

I2P Stats
http://stats.i2p
I2P Stats displays statistics for I2P. Useful for research into dark web platforms, I2P Stats will be discussed in more detail in chapter 8.

I2P Forum
http://forum.i2p
I2P forum is the main discussion forum for I2P. It is moderated but not censored for content (except that pertaining to domestic/child abuse).

Anoncoin
http://anoncoin.i2p
Anoncoin was first produced in 2013. It is one of the more affordable cryptocurrencies available on the web and was developed for I2P.[14] Through this site you can purchase and sell the currency or use the currency to purchase goods and services. Is it not nearly as popular as Bitcoin, but works using the same principles. The virtual "currency" is in fact a unique segment of code that is traded, with transactions anonymously logged. Cryptocurrency, how it works, and its relationship to the dark web will be discussed in greater detail in chapter 7.

Echelon
http://echelon.i2p
Echelon provides all the major developer updates for I2P.

Exchanged
http://exchanged.i2p
Exchanged is a major exchange site for cryptocurrencies. It includes stock tickers for various cryptocurrencies, including current prices in Bitcoin and USD. It also

includes a marketplace for purchasing Bitcoin and nine other major cryptocurrencies, using official currency from fifteen nations worldwide (including USD). Prices range from a few dollars for lesser known cryptocurrencies up to several thousand USD for a single Bitcoin.

I2P Bug Tracker
http://trac.i2p.i2p/report/1
I2P Bug Tracker monitors all bugs and bug fixes in I2P. It provides references for any users who experience challenges with I2P.

I2P FAQ
http://i2p-projekt.i2p/en/faq
The Frequently Asked Questions section of I2P can address most of the issues novice users may encounter with the platform.

I2P Wiki
http://i2pwiki.i2p/
A wiki for I2P. I2P Wiki is not as expansive as Wikipedia, but provides sufficient information about most of the major features and sites on I2P.

Planet I2P
http://planet.i2p
Planet I2P is a general newsfeed for I2P. It contains information from developers as well as users. Planet I2P has several different feeds (listed on the right side of the page) and is sorted based on date of post.

The Tin Hat
http://secure.thetinhat.i2p/
The Tin Hat contains a wide variety of tutorials and articles on topics of interest to dark web users. Topics range from Bitcoin to WhatsApp to ransomware to secure email. The hallmark of the Tin Hat is straight, no-bull answers from experts. No sensationalism.

Plug-ins

I2Phex
i2phex.su3; i2phex-windows.su3
I2Phex is a file sharing plug-in that emulates the file sharing capabilities of Freenet.

Syndie
http://syndie.su3
Syndie is a secure message board for I2P.

Seedless
http://sponge.i2p
Seedless is a popular platform for I2P file distribution.

CONCLUSION

Because there is no Google for the dark web, navigation can be a difficult task. This chapter serves as a guide to the sites of the dark web and how to access them. This enables the reader to understand and evaluate the content of sites before viewing them. It enables organizations to determine for what purposes the sites should and should not be used by patrons. The following two chapters will explore legal and ethical issues surrounding these sites, as well as how the sites may be used to support human rights and scholarly research.

NOTES

1. David M. Goldschlag, Michael G. Reed, and Paul F. Syverson, "Privacy on the Internet," Onion-Router.net, April 17, 1997, https://www.onion-router.net/Publications/INET-1997.html.

2. Michael G. Reed, Paul F. Syverson, and David M. Goldschlag, "Proxies for Anonymous Routing," Proceedings of the 12th Annual Computer Security Applications Conference (San Diego, CA, 1996), 95–104.

3. Roger Dingledine, Nick Mathewson, and Paul Syverson, "Tor: The Second-Generation Onion Router," Defense Technical Information Center, January 2004, https://apps.dtic.mil/dtic/tr/fulltext/u2/a465464.pdf.

4. The Tor Project, "Onion Services," accessed June 6, 2018, https://metrics.torproject.org/hidserv-dir-onions-seen.html.

5. Cynthia G. Giwa, "Why ProPublica Joined the Dark Web," January 19, 2016, https://www.propublica.org/podcast/why-propublica-joined-the-dark-web.

6. Alec Muffet, "1 Million People Use Facebook over Tor," April 22, 2016, https://www.facebook.com/notes/facebook-over-tor/1-million-people-use-facebook-over-tor/865624066877648/.

7. Kate Murphy, "Should All Research Papers Be Free?" *New York Times*, March 12, 2016, https://www.nytimes.com/2016/03/13/opinion/sunday/should-all-research-papers-be-free.html.

8. Robert Johnson, "A 'Deep Web' Guide to the Secret Tunnels under Virginia Tech," *Business Insider*, April 24, 2013, www.businessinsider.com/tunnels-beneath-virginia-tech-2013-4.

9. David Kushner, "Dead End on Silk Road: Internet Crime Kingpin Ross Ulbricht's Big Fall," *Rolling Stone*, February 4, 2014, https://www.rollingstone.com/culture/news/dead-end-on-silk-road-Internet-crime-kingpin-ross-ulbrichts-big-fall-20140204.

10. Nathaniel Popper, "The Tax Sleuth Who Took Down a Drug Lord," *New York Times*, December 25, 2015, https://www.nytimes.com/2015/12/27/business/dealbook/the-unsung-tax-agent-who-put-a-face-on-the-silk-road.html.

11. Samuel Gibbs, "Swedish Police Raid Sinks the Pirate Bay," *Guardian*, December 10, 2014, https://www.theguardian.com/technology/2014/dec/10/swedish-police-raid-pirate-bay.

12. Peter Conrad, "Free communications on the Freenet Network," Accessed July 14, 2018, http://www.linux-magazine.com/Issues/2008/91/Freenet.

13. Elsevier et al. v. Sci-Hub et al., 15 Civ. 4282 (New York, 2015).

14. Anoncoin, "About Anoncoin," July 17, 2018, https://anoncoin.net/About_Anoncoin/.

7

Legal and Ethical Issues with the Dark Web

HISTORY OF LEGAL AND ETHICAL ISSUES ON THE DARK WEB

The earliest mentions of illegal activity on dark web–type networks predate even Tor. Proto-dark web platforms—similar in appearance to Freenet—were developed in the early 2000s to temporarily exchange information between criminal groups.[1] These platforms were not nearly as advanced (or secure) as the platforms used today. Most were not "dark" at all and could be easily shut down.

As the dark web evolved, so did the criminal activity. Direct peer-to-peer file sharing and communication were used throughout the first decade of the 2000s. In most cases, the dark web networks were used only to negotiate a deal that would then be completed in person.[2] The dark web was simply a facilitator for communication, not unlike the burner phones and pagers depicted famously in the HBO television show *The Wire*.

Throughout the early and mid-2000s, the dark web remained relatively low on the criminality radar. It was still known mostly for its association with the military and had low use among the public. The traditional World Wide Web was not nearly as intrusive on the privacy of users as it is today. It was possible to maintain an illegal network on the web for months before it was shut down, often with little more than a slap on the wrist for perpetrators. It was not until the time of Chelsea Manning, Edward Snowden, and Aaron Swartz in the mid- and late 2000s that surveillance and shutdowns became widespread.

Table 7.1. Timeline of Major Dark Web Releases and Shutdowns

2002	Tor is released for public use
2010	Farmer's Market is released on Tor
2011	Silk Road is launched on Tor
April 2012	Farmer's Market is shut down by international law enforcement
October 2013	Silk Road is shut down by the FBI
November 2014	Silk Road 2.0 is shut down by law enforcement; Silk Road 3.0 launches
February 2017	Silk Road 3.0 folds due to insufficient funds; subsequent sites are limited in size and scope

The first proto-marketplace to enter the dark web was Farmer's Market. Farmer's Market operated on the World Wide Web from 2006 to 2010, serving as a kind of chat forum for the exchange of illicit drugs.[3] At the time it was little more than the peer-to-peer communication forums operating on the dark web. In 2010 the site was transferred to Tor, where services could be provided more openly. Unfortunately for Farmer's Market users, when the DEA decided to pursue the network and its users, the data from the pre-Tor days was easily accessible. From 2010 to 2012 the DEA tracked thousands and arrested dozens of individuals who used the site.[4]

The first true dark web marketplace was Silk Road. This site offered a full-fledged buy-sell market with business conducted entirely online. It was an Amazon for the illegal. Silk Road was launched in February 2011 and in just two and a half years was responsible for $1.2 billion in transactions.[5] The floodgates had been opened that would give the dark web its unfortunate moniker.

Following the success of Silk Road, several similar sites appeared on Tor, including Black Market Reloaded and Sheep Marketplace. Atlantis Marketplace was late to the scene, founded only in March 2013, just months before the major DEA crackdown on dark web marketplaces. Atlantis, however, was revolutionary for being the first dark web marketplace to accept the cryptocurrency Bitcoin.[6] It is regarded by many researchers as the reason for the initial emergence of Bitcoin internationally.

CRYPTOCURRENCY AND THE DARK WEB

The story of cryptocurrency, in general, parallels that of the dark web, with both only recently gaining mainstream interest. Though cryptocurrency is not the subject of this book, it so intertwines with the dark web that it is worth discussing in some detail.

Cryptocurrency is a type of currency that meets the following conditions:

- Runs independent of a central authority
- Contains cryptographic elements, meaning that a certain anonymity is ensured (discussed below)
- A system (rather than an individual or group) defines whether and when new elements can be created, thus controlling inflation

Cryptocurrency is a code (or "key") that is associated with an individual's pseudonymous "wallet" (similar to a bank account number). The amount of currency held in users' wallets is tracked in a ledger, which is a type of shared spreadsheet (i.e., a spreadsheet in which everyone can see how much currency everyone else has in their accounts).

A transaction occurs when a certain amount of currency is transferred from one user to another. This is tracked by broadcasting the account numbers of the two users making the transaction. The validity of a transaction is maintained by entering the private key along with the public account numbers, which are then validated using algorithms developed by the cryptocurrency system and verified by other users worldwide.

A Simplified Look at a BitCoin Transaction

Xq121x3	56.23BTC	0.89 BTC to 90Ji0e4	Xq12x3	55.34BTC
90Ji0e4	1.39BTC	0.89 BTC from Xq12x3	90Ji0e4	2.28BTC
Y969qS5	*12BTC*		*Y969qS5*	*12 BTC*

Fortunately for the average user, the front-end process is no different than using a credit card to make a purchase.

How does this tie into the dark web and illegal activity? There are no names associated with account numbers and the money system is decentralized (thousands of users have copies of the ledger), meaning it is difficult to track a user down or to seize his account.

Table 7.2.   Economic Impact of Silk Road. Total Value of Silk Road Transactions (2011–2013): 9,519,664 Bitcoins

Month and Year	Value of Bitcoin	Value of Silk Road's Total Transactions Based on Bitcoin Exchange Rates	Percent Change (+/–)
September 2010	$0.12	$1 Million	–
February 2011	$1	$10 Million	733%
July 2011	$30	$285 Million	2900%
December 2011	$3	$20 Million	–90%
May 2012	$5	$48 Million	66%
October 2012	$9	$86 Million	80%
February 2013	$40	$381 Million	344%
March 2013	$115	$1.1 Billion	188%
April 2013	$250	$2.4 Billion	117%
May 2013	$140	$1.3 Billion	–44%
June 2013	$100	$952 Million	–29%
July 2013	$80	$752 Million	–20%
August 2013	$90	$857 Million	13%
September 2013	$120	$1.2 Billion	33%
October 2013	$120	$1.2 Billion	–
Early November 2013	$200	$1.9 Billion	67%
Late November 2013	$400	$3.8 Billion	100%
Early December 2013	$500	$4.8 Billion	25%
Mid December 2013	$1,200	$11.4 Billion	140%
Late December 2013	$600	$5.7 Billion	–50%
January 2014	$800	$7.6 Billion	33%
February 2014	$700	$6.7 Billion	–13%
Peak 2015	$500	$4.8 Billion	–40%
Peak 2016	$800	$7.6 Billion	60%
Peak 2017	$18,000	$171.4 Billion	2150%
Peak 2018	$10,000	$95.2 Billion	–44%
End of 2018	$3,500	$33.3 Billion	–65%*

*Bitcoin has lost 81% of its total value from its peak in 2017. Someone who invested $100 in Bitcoin in 2017 would have only $19 today. However, those who invested $100 at the start of Bitcoin in 2010 would be worth nearly $3 million today (a 30,000% increase).

In the wake of initial shutdowns of the major dark web marketplaces in late 2013, a new crop almost immediately emerged. Among these were Silk Road 2.0—run by some of the surviving developers from the original Silk Road project—Cloud 9, and Hydra. However, now that a strategy for attacking the sites' vulnerabilities had emerged, the DEA was quick to pursue the new marketplaces.

From November 5 to 7, 2014, dozens of dark web sites were shut down and seventeen arrests were made in what would be known as Operation Onymous.[7] This operation essentially ended the era of the major dark web marketplace. Though a Silk Road 3.0 opened immediately after the shutdown of Silk Road 2.0, it floundered financially, as did attempts to resurrect the other sites. Illicit activities receded into the smaller corners of the dark web as more legitimate sites came to the fore.

On a different note, a second group of "illegal" activity emerged during the early 2010s. This was the product of hacktivists and whistleblowers like Anonymous, Aaron Swartz, and Edward Snowden. The legality (or at least morality) of these figures is highly controversial, especially among information professionals. Many regard these individuals as Robin Hood-esque figures, while the government often portrays them as treasonous.

Swartz, in particular, was crucial in developing several key fixtures of the dark web. He coproduced the platform SecureDrop, which runs on Tor and provides a medium for whistleblowers to communicate information to the press. Currently, the *New Yorker*, *Forbes*, Associated Press, *New York Times*, *USA Today*, and *Wall Street Journal* all participate in SecureDrop. This platform has received scrutiny particularly from the executive branch of the United States government.

Swartz was arrested in 2011 after authorities accused him of downloading millions of articles from the JSTOR scholarly database, allegedly with the intent to distribute the articles online free of charge. Swartz was charged on eleven total counts including wire fraud, computer fraud, unlawfully obtaining information from a protected computer, and recklessly damaging a protected computer.[8] Before he was scheduled to appear for trial in January 2013, Swartz committed suicide in his New York apartment.

Illegal content is certainly still on the dark web, but not nearly in the concentration that it was in the early 2010s. In fact, many of the "black sites" that are online today are scam sites and joke sites posted to try to get users to reveal personal information. While there are many small illegal sites, there are no huge organizations like Silk Road any longer. This makes the dark web much more navigable for the average user who wishes to avoid illegal activity during their browsing experience.

EXAMPLES OF THE ILLEGAL
CONTENT AVAILABLE ON THE DARK WEB

There are several categories of illegal content available on the dark web, many of which are also available on the World Wide Web through various chat rooms but are not as well publicized. These categories range from malware, account information, and fake passports and citizenship documents to weapons, illicit drugs, and money-laundering services to abusive pornography.

Much of the alleged illegal content on the dark web today is a hoax. For instance, there have been no confirmed successful assassination schemes. There are certainly many websites that claim to offer murder for hire, but these are mostly created in jest. The Assassination Market (assmkedzgorodn7o.onion) is an example of a site that has been in place since 2013 but has never successfully led to any assassinations. Is this illegal and inappropriate? The argument can certainly be made. Is it real? Usually not.

How Governments and Other Users Are Cracking Down on
Criminals Using the Dark Web

Though you may technically be anonymous on the dark web, that does not mean you cannot be apprehended for illegal behavior. There are several ways that government authorities and self-policing users can help shut down illegal sites and identify criminals. Many of these stem back to traditional detective methods. Others take plays from the hackers' handbook.

The most effective method used to bust criminals is good old-fashioned undercover work. Criminals are frequently lolled into a sense of security on the dark web and may use real names or email addresses while making purchases, believing that there is no way for external entities to access the information. Unfortunately for them, authorities are frequently on the other side of the transaction. This method serves as a deterrent for potential criminals—that they might trust the platform but cannot trust the person on the other side.

Investigators will also pose as allies and programmers, infiltrating the top levels of organizations and collecting as much information as possible about the organization, its administrators, and its users before initiating a major crackdown. They serve essentially an informant role. It is easy to think the stories about such individuals are fictionalized, but infiltration—along with surveillance and malware—is responsible for most of the major shutdowns discussed at the opening of this chapter.[9]

Investigating forums is a particularly useful method to identify criminals. Criminals like to brag of their feats and to ask for help. If they let up their cover and reveal any personal information, it can be enough to ignite a massive investigation. An excellent example of this is the takedown of Silk Road.

Finally, investigators may use malware to identify criminals and shut down websites. Malware is a type of malicious software that when introduced to a computer causes some type of damage. The malware may be designed to gather information about the site and its users or compromise a computer. This software is often initiated through a download. On the dark web this has been used widely and with great success to catch those attempting to download illegal pornography.[10]

So what can you, as a dark web user, do to assist in identifying and apprehending criminals? As in the offline world, always report anything suspicious. However, understand that dark web crimes often will not be a topic that the local police will understand. Instead, this information can be reported directly to the FBI (https://www.fbi.gov/tips).

Ethical Issues on the Dark Web

While illegal content on the dark web has declined significantly over the past half decade, unethical content is a different story. Unethical content is described here as that which is legal but which some might deem in poor taste. Violent videos and legal pornography are two examples. Depending on where you look, this content can be relatively regular.

According to at least one source, up to 60 percent of the content on the dark web may be unethical.[11] How does this compare to the World Wide Web? Of the top fifty websites for the year 2017, as identified by Alexa Internet, we identified thirty-two (64 percent) allow some type of content that could be deemed unethical (e.g., do not censor legal, illicit content).[12] Eight of the most popular websites tailor to "unethical" content specifically (mostly legal pornography sites).

Necessity breeds change and unethical people will be unethical. When a platform presents itself that can preserve the identity of unethical people as they conduct illicit affairs, they will flock to it quickly and innovate. Meanwhile, the mainstream will not immediately recognize the value of the platform. Thus, it is like taming the Wild West. The more ethical users there are, the less impact unethical users will have on the platform.

Like on the World Wide Web, the content you get depends on where you look and for what you are looking. Just as with searching Google, imprecise browsing on the dark web may lead to unintended results. As discussed in the previous chapter, knowing what you are looking for, maintaining an index of sites, and avoiding randomly wandering the dark web will reduce the likelihood that you happen upon content you do not wish to view.

HOW TO AVOID ILLEGAL CONTENT ON THE DARK WEB

How do you make sure that you do not accidentally run into illegal content while browsing the dark web for legitimate reasons?

One benefit about not having a search engine to rely on as a crutch is that you are unlikely to just happen upon a site with illegal content. In most cases the people who find themselves on these sites know exactly why they are there. Tor sites do not have obvious names like illegalstuff.onion.

A useful practice is to create an individualized catalog for favorite sites. This can be done in one of two ways: by saving the pages in Tor, or by creating a spreadsheet catalog.

To save sites within Tor, simply click on "Settings" (the three horizontal bars at the top right of the browser), then click "Bookmarks" and "Bookmark this page." This is certainly the easiest method to save sites, but also leaves the content vulnerable should the physical computer become compromised.

The second, more secure method to save sites is by creating a password-protected spreadsheet. This also allows the user to enter additional metadata, such as website name, description of the site, etc. If an organization was to provide access to the dark web, making a public version of such a spreadsheet may prove immensely beneficial to users and provide direction as to "approved" sites.

But what if you want to find some new sites to visit? All three major dark web platforms have aggregated lists of sites that avoid illegal content. An example of this is Freenet's Filtered Index. Another useful system is using the World Wide Web or dark web wiki to look up more information about a site before visiting it.

What if you happen upon a site that contains illegal content? You can report the site and its content to the FBI, especially if you think others may come across it unwittingly, though it is possible the bureau may already know about it. Some of the dark web platforms will also allow you to block a site. Within Tor, for instance, you can download an add-on that will allow you to block sites of your choosing. This feature can help ensure that you do not accidentally happen upon the site again. (The feature is discussed further in the following section.)

LIMITING OTHERS' ACCESS TO
ILLEGAL CONTENT ON THE DARK WEB

The topic of limiting or monitoring how individuals within an organization use the dark web is challenging. Many public and school libraries take part in the E-rate Internet discount program, which requires them to adhere to the Children's Internet Protection Act (CIPA). This legislation requires filtering software to be placed on all computers that blocks access to images that are obscene or harmful to minors.[13] They must also enforce an "Internet safety policy."

CIPA does seemingly allow for patron use of the dark web, at least for adult patrons. Section 254(h) paragraph 6, subsection B and C of the Communications Act of 1934, as revised by the passage of CIPA, states that libraries with more than one computer having Internet access . . .:

> (i) is enforcing a policy of Internet safety that includes the operation of a technology protection measure with respect to any of its computers with Internet access that protects against access through such computers to visual depictions that are—
> (I) obscene;
> (II) child pornography; or
> (III) harmful to minors; and
> (ii) is enforcing the operation of such technology protection measure during any use of such computers by minors.

According to the American Library Association, "An administrator, supervisor, or other person authorized by the school or library may disable the filtering software during use by an adult, to enable access for bona fide research or for another lawful purpose."[14]

In other words, adult patrons may use the dark web so long as they are using it for legal means. Any illegal activity uncovered from the patron may be reported to law enforcement. As a secondary measure, libraries/organizations can reduce their culpability for the online activity of patrons by adopting an Internet policy that guides appropriate dark web use. As part of the policy, the organization may list types of content that are allowed or list specific sites (Facebook, ProPublica, WikiLeaks) that are acceptable for users to access via the dark web. Organizations (and individuals, for that matter) can also filter the dark web, as discussed in the following text box. Libraries and schools, however, should check with an E-rate administrator before assuming that these filters will satisfy the stipulation of CIPA.

FILTERING THE DARK WEB

Organizations that are subject to CIPA regulations, or those that just want to bar access to certain dark web sites, may install a web filter. These filters are not 100 percent effective and the content that the user could be exposed to if the filter fails is more severe, so organizations that are required to filter certain content should check with officials before assuming the filter is sufficient.

One of the best keyword-based filters is Procon Latte. This is an add-on that can be downloaded for the Tor browser free of charge. Procon will block sites with certain keywords in their titles or content and censor words from a list. On Tor the filter will block both WWW and dark web sites based on the keywords. The filter can be locked using password protection, so it can be used effectively with organizations as well as personal computers. This will allow you to still use the dark web without accidentally accessing illegal sites. Users should be aware, however, that the plug-in can collect information about the user and thus does affect privacy. That said, we recommend Procon as a compromise for organizations seeking to provide access to Tor.

There are also content-based filters, such as Fox Filter and Parental Control, which are typically designed for Firefox but work on Tor and are available in the Tor plug-in collection. These filters can identify content and block only specific pages, which preserves access to sites that are improperly blocked by keyword filters.

On I2P and Freenet there are less robust options. Most are third-party plug-ins and have varying levels of effectiveness. These can be added in respective plug-in stores.

While there is no penalty for entering the address of a dark web site that includes illegal content, any action taken on the site (clicking on a link or viewing an image, up to making a purchase or download) can come with a legal penalty based on content. As many libraries and organizations already do—by posting copyright infringement notices—information can be publicly displayed pertaining to certain activities and their associated penalties. Here are a few examples of crimes that might be committed on the dark web and their associated federal penalties:

- Wire fraud (as defined in 18 US Code 1343 "Fraud by wire/radio/television")
  - Definition: To defraud or obtain money by means of false pretenses, representations, or promises, by means of any writing, signs, signals, pictures or sounds

- o Plain-language definition: To trick others into giving you money without fulfilling your side of the transaction
- o Penalty: Fine and/or maximum twenty-year imprisonment for each count
- Computer fraud (as defined by 18 US Code 1030 "Fraud and related acts in connection with computer")
  - o Definition: To access a computer without authorization or *exceeding authorized access*
  - o Plain-language definition: Using a computer for some purpose other than that which the organization allows/accessing private content
  - o Penalty: A fine and/or imprisonment of no more than ten years for each count
- Copyright infringement (as defined by 17 US Code 506 "Criminal infringement")
  - o Definition: Any person who willingly infringes copyright for financial gain, or distributes a work meant for commercial distribution
  - o Plain-language definition: Selling or providing for free any material that is not owned by you
  - o Penalty: Fine and/or maximum of ten years imprisonment depending on infringement type
- Sexual abuse of children or protected persons (as defined by 18 US Code 1466 "Obscene visual representations")
  - o Definition: Distributing or viewing any depictions of the sexual abuse of children, or mentally disabled persons
  - o Penalty: Fine and imprisonment of no less than five years and no more than twenty years
- Tax evasion (as defined by 26 US Code 7201 "Attempt to evade or defeat tax")
  - o Definition: Any person who willfully attempts in any manner to evade or defeat any tax imposed by this title or the payment thereof
  - o Plain-language definition: As most illegal dark web purchases do not pay tax (for obvious reasons), tax evasion is the most common way to punish those who engage in these activities
  - o Penalty: Fine of no more than $100,000 plus the costs of prosecution and/or imprisonment of no more than five years

CAN THE DARK WEB BE
TAKEN DOWN? WHY YOU SHOULD CARE

While the dark web likely can never be completely taken down, many attempts have been made to compromise part of the network, some of which have succeeded. Due to its popularity and notoriety, Tor has been the focus of a number of attacks. These range from legitimate attacks by individuals hoping to exploit the system, to vulnerability testing by researchers, to censorship attempts by governments and political groups.

DOES THE DARK WEB DO MORE HARM THAN GOOD?

Throughout this book we have painted the dark web in a positive light—because we want to convince you that it's something worth preserving (which we wholeheartedly believe). However, we don't want to make it seem as though something is being swept under the rug. So here are some straight facts on the dark side of the dark web:

- According to a report by Moore and Rid (2016) over one-half of dark web sites contain illicit content.[15]
- Malware is sold on the dark web that can be used to hack servers and companies. One such malware package was used in the Target stores credit card breach of 2013, which exposed the credit card information of millions of customers.
- Nearly $100 million in illegal goods are sold on the dark web each year.

Do we believe that these facts illustrate that the dark web does more harm than good? No. Just as the Wild West was once rife with criminals and oddballs of all sorts before being tamed by an influx of law-abiding people, we believe the dark web can be tamed by an influx of legitimate users. The benefits of privacy and security, in a world that seems to have increasingly less of both, are direly needed.

An early successful attempt to compromise Tor was the work of computer security consultant Dan Egerstad. Egerstad's efforts focused on the exit relay of the dark web connection, the final step before the router connects to a website.[16] In hosting exit relays, Egerstad was able to see any World Wide Web content run on the browser.[17] This exposed hundreds of individuals who used Tor to access email accounts and work logins on the Tor network. This data could have likely been sold for tens of thousands of dollars, had Egerstad not collected the data only for research purposes. The incident brought focus to existing privacy concerns on Tor. It also brought attention to the need for responsible, ethical standards of exit relays. Ideally, an exit relay would not be run by an individual but rather an organization that is dedicated to preserving privacy, such as a library.

Rob Jansen (of the US Naval Research Laboratory) and his colleagues describe a method for completely disabling the Tor network and deanonymizing all the platform's users.[18] The so-called Sniper attack would deploy a type of denial of service (DOS) attack across the entire Tor network. A denial of service attack is a cyberattack in which a system is flooded with access requests, overloading the system and preventing legitimate access requests. Imagine you need to visit the DMV and your enemy really wants to make your life a pain, so he gathers a hundred volunteers to line up at the DMV in front of you and waste time. The DMV will be so busy with these fraudulent customers that they will not be able to serve your legitimate need. That's a denial of service attack: flooding the line at the DMV so that you can't get in. This method is very common in cyberattacks, especially those of the group Anonymous during its peak in the early 2010s.

The idea of the Sniper attack is to conduct a denial of service attack against Tor, flooding the legitimate exit relays (as discussed with Egerstad's case) and leaving the traffic to either have no access to Tor or—possibly even worse—only access through exit relays run by the attackers, which would be set up to collect as much of the users' data as possible. This type of attack would undoubtedly have a long-term impact and might shatter trust in the platform. Fortunately, the researchers on this study—as most dark web researchers do—worked with Tor to construct a solution to this vulnerability. The prospect of such an attack, however, emphasizes the need for a large and robust distribution of dark web relays across the globe, all dedicated to preserving the privacy of users.

Attacks against Freenet and I2P are less common, as the platforms are simply less robust but also more secure in what they do. That does not mean that vulnerabilities do not exist. One cyberattack that is common among all of these anonymity platforms is the Sybil attack.[19] The Sybil attack is named after the case of Sybil, a woman diagnosed with multiple personalities (dissociative identity disorder). In a Sybil attack, the attackers create a large number of accounts, with the effect of a small group wielding a disproportionate amount of power. This can be used on the World Wide Web to rig online votes and organization ratings (and, unfortunately, very often is used to influence potentially important outcomes). On the dark web peer-to-peer networks, the Sybil attack functions very similarly to the denial of service attack by flooding the network and making it essentially unusable. While some solutions have been put in place to prevent Sybil attacks, they are still quite ubiquitous. This presents a serious ethical dilemma for developers of dark web sites, who do not want to censor legitimate traffic but want to prevent Sybil attacks. It is also something for users to look for and try to report to site administrators as quickly as possible.

Understanding potential threats to the dark web is important to include in this chapter on legal and ethical considerations because it is possible that a group that might wish to initiate one of these attacks morally or legally objects to the network's content. It is important to gather from this chapter that the dark web is not intended to be dark in an evil sense and the positive aspects of the dark web platforms far outweigh the negatives. You, as potential users of dark web services, hosts of dark web relays, and supporters of dark web adoption, can serve an important role in preventing a coordinated attack through the power of education. That is the role of this book: to educate you so that you may educate others.

To keep up to date on threats to the dark web platforms, make sure to subscribe to the newsletter provided by Tor, follow the platforms' social media accounts, and regularly check their websites for updates. All of the platforms have a presence at major academic conferences on privacy. All provide diverse opportunities to volunteer. Staying informed and involved will make you the first line of defense against any attacks.

CONCLUSION

One of the most—if not *the* most—pervasive myths about the dark web is that it is only used by and intended for criminals. While the platform has unfortunately been host to illegal content throughout its existence, this is not the mission of the dark web but an unfortunate side effect. With proper policing by the dark web community and an influx of new law-abiding users, the influence of illegal activity can be significantly reduced and the dark web can fulfill its intended goals. These goals and the steps to satisfy them will be discussed extensively in chapter 8.

NOTES

1. Matthew Warren and William Hutchinson, "The Use of the Internet by Terrorists," *Journal of the Australian Institute of Professional Intelligence Officers* 10, no. 2 (2002): 17–28.

2. Wojciech Filipkowski, "Internet as an Illegal Marketplace," presented at the Sixth Colloquium on Cross-Border Crime (Berlin, Germany, 2004).

3. Julia Buxton and Tim Bingham, "The Rise and Challenge of Dark Net Drug Markets," Global Drug Policy Observatory Policy Brief 7 (January 2015), https://www.swansea.ac.uk/media/The%20Rise%20and%20Challenge%20of%20Dark%20Net%20Drug%20Markets.pdf.

4. United States of America v. Marc Peter Willems et al., CR 11 01137 (California 2011).

5. Steve Kovach, "FBI Says Illegal Drugs Marketplace Silk Road Generated $1.2 Billion in Sales Revenue," October 2, 2013, https://www.businessinsider.com/silk-road-revenue-2013-10.

6. Andy Greenberg, "Bitcoin Black Market Competition Heats Up, with Pro Marketing and Millions at Stake," *Forbes*, June 26, 2013, https://www.forbes.com/sites/andygreenberg/2013/06/26/bitcoin-black-market-competition-heats-up-with-pro-marketing-and-millions-at-stake/#85dad87e2f23.

7. United Nations Office on Drugs and Crime, "Operation Onymous," December 1, 2017, https://www.unodc.org/cld/case-law-doc/cybercrimecrimetype/xxx/operation_onymous.html.

8. United States v. Swartz, 1:11-cr-10260, 160 (2013).

9. Federal Bureau of Investigation, "Operation Disarray: Shining a Light on the Dark Web," April 3, 2018, https://www.fbi.gov/news/stories/operation-disarray-040318.

10. Federal Bureau of Investigation, "The Dark Web," October 17, 2014, https://www.fbi.gov/audio-repository/news-podcasts-thisweek-the-dark-web.mp3/view.

11. Gareth Owen and Nick Savage, "The Tor Dark Net," Global Commission on Internet Governance Paper Series, no. 20 (September 2015), https://www.cigionline.org/sites/default/files/no20_0.pdf.

12. Alexa Internet, Inc., "The Top 500 Sites on the Web," accessed May 3, 2018, https://www.alexa.com/topsites.

13. Federal Communications Commission, "Children's Internet Protection Act," accessed June 1, 2018, https://www.fcc.gov/consumers/guides/childrens-internet-protection-act.

14. American Library Association, "CIPA Legal FAQ," accessed Februrary 22, 2018, http://www.ala.org/advocacy/advleg/federallegislation/cipa/cipalegalfaq.

15. Daniel Moore and Thomas Rid, "Cryptopolitik and the Darknet," *Survival* 58, no. 1 (2016): 7–38.

16. Kim Zetter, "Rogue Nodes Turn Tor Anonymizer into Eavesdropper's Paradise," *Wired*, September 10, 2007, https://www.wired.com/2007/09/rogue-nodes-turn-tor-anonymizer-into-eavesdroppers-paradise/.

17. Patrick Gray, "Embassy Hacker Dan Egerstad and the Tor Network," *Computer Weekly*, December 3, 2007, https://www.computerweekly.com/news/2240022106/Embassy-hacker-Dan-Egerstad-and-the-Tor-network.

18. Rob Jansen, Florian Tschorsch, Aaron Johnson, and Bjorn Scheuermann, "The Sniper Attack: Anonymously Deanonymizing and Disabling the Tor Network," February 2014, http://www.robgjansen.com/publications/sniper-ndss2014.pdf.

19. Christoph Egger, Johannes Schlumberger, Christopher Kruegel, and Giovanni Vigna, "Practical Attacks against the I2P Network," 2013, https://www.cs.ucsb.edu/~chris/research/doc/raid13_i2p.pdf.

8

Research and Advocacy on the Dark Web

On the surface, it might seem that the only incentive for the average Internet user to use the dark web is enhanced privacy or illegal activities. But there are many legitimate uses of the dark web. From research, advocacy, and infrastructure support to smart financial and developmental investments, the dark web offers many incentives beyond just privacy. Here are just a few examples of ways for individuals and organizations to truly reap the rewards of the dark web.

DARK WEB RESEARCH

The Authors' Research

If you will indulge us briefly, so that we may impress the PhDs (or at least act like we know what we are talking about when we honestly have no clue), we would like to discuss our own research approach for this book and a bit about why we thought it was important to write it. Our approach to research and crafting a narrative within this book is informed by our quasi-postmodernist outlook of the social world—it would be safe to suggest that we tilt toward the paradigm of radical change and are inspired by Deleuze and Foucault (the Tupac of philosophy)—which leads us to question established narratives about the dark web. We build this book off of our personal experience, source documents, and dialogue with other users of the dark web. We push back against the functionalist forms of thought that maintain status quo and resist the democratizing power of the dark web.

Our approach to distilling this information about the dark web is heavily influenced by our understanding of the adaptation and diffusion of knowledge, based on the work of Everett Rogers.[1] We could write a dry, boring academic text on the dark web, but who would want to read it? We sure would not. So, we took the important information and are communicating it in an enjoyable and approachable way. We do not believe this degrades the quality of our research throughout the book, which, you can believe, was extremely thorough. This has also led us to reference the primary source documents (e.g., the original publications written by Syverson, Reed, and Goldschlag) rather than what others have written (though we referred to both throughout the preparation of this book).

Insomuch as we have tried to align this book to our background as library and information science researchers and professionals, we have used the American Library Association's Core Values of Librarianship to guide our work.[2] We have sought to encourage proactive service in information privacy and security, following the library service models described by Greer, Grover, and Fowler.[3] We believe we are building on a tradition of information science usability and knowledge diffusion research that dates back to Vannevar Bush, Robert S. Taylor, and Jesse Shera (obligatory name-drops). We thought it was important to share our theoretical lenses and associated assumptions here to let the reader know that we made a conscious decision to combine evidence-based research, primary source documents, firsthand narratives, and personal experience with engaging prose. We also want to point out to the potential dark web research where we believe the current research is lacking—namely, in its primarily functionalist/scientist agenda. Our success at adhering to any of these paradigms we discuss ultimately varies throughout the book, because our greatest aim is always to present information in a way that is easy to read and enjoyable for all without bogging the book down with needless jargon or philosophical asides.

Platform Statistics

There are two major ways to conduct research on/about the dark web. The first is by using the analytics provided by Tor, Freenet, and I2P (quantitative research). The second is through using the platforms themselves for content analysis and action research (mostly qualitative).

Tor Metrics

Tor Metrics (metrics.torproject.org) offers thousands of statistics and analyses on the use of its platform (all anonymized, of course).[4] Tor Metrics divides its statistical analysis tools into the categories of analysis and services. These are subsequently divided into multiple subcategories. The subcategories of analysis include breakdowns based on:

- Users: includes data on total users on Tor dating back to mid-2011 as well as the number of users by country, the top countries for users, and lists of possible censorship events
- Servers: provides statistics on the relay nodes
- Traffic: offers estimates of total bandwidth used by Tor as well as bandwidth distribution
- Performance: lists the average time to download files over Tor as well as the number of timeouts and failures of downloading files over Tor
- Onion services: shows the total number of unique .onion addresses and onion-service traffic
- Applications: displays the number of Tor browser downloads and updates as well as the number of Tor downloads by platform (Windows, Mac, Linux)

The subcategories of services include:

- Relay search: allows users to search information on specific Tor relays
- Aggregated relay search: similar to relay search but reports on a group of relays
- Network archive: enables users to look up whether an IP address has been used as a Tor relay

Using Tor Metrics, you can compare overall Tor relay users (overall users) by country versus Tor bridge users (users who seek an additional layer of security). For instance, from March 2015 to 2018, the top five overall users of Tor were the United States, Germany, Russia, the United Arab Emirates, and France, but the top five bridge users during that period were Russia, the United States, the United Arab Emirates, Iran, and Turkey. You can also view the Oxford Internet Institute's "The Anonymous Internet" cartographic representation of dark web use.[5]

Freenet Statistics

Freenet Statistics provides fairly detailed information on the platform, with descriptions of what each statistic means. Once Freenet is installed on your computer, it can be found at http://localhost:8888/USK@WMa1Z40iYdZZ51yctQ3toFl9zuuFE nNdsm3NejJU5KE,jCBcaNBeKD5~sSQeSkyKz737Bh5ibBGqdzfD8mgfdMY,AQ ACAAE/statistics/213/.

These stats can be a bit more difficult to decipher than the Tor Metrics, so let us break down each section.

- Network size: equal to the number of nodes or relays in the network. Hourly instantaneous shows how many relays are running at a particular time, whereas the effective size is the number of unique relays to run during a given period. This is then, of course, a good predictor of the strength of the network.
- Datastore size: represents the total storage of information on the platform. This is often measured in terabytes (one trillion bytes or one thousand gigabytes).
- Errors and refused: as evident in the name, this measures issues that occur within the platform. Most of these are overload errors (asking the platform to do too much too quickly).
- Peer count: a measure of the number of connections using a certain node and what percent of nodes have that many connections
- Link length: describes the average length of connections between nodes
- Uptime distribution: displays the amount of time a node is "up" during a given time period
- Bulk reject: indicates the health of a network. A Freenet node will refuse to allow a user to connect if they lack sufficient bandwidth.

Freenet statistics have remained fairly consistent over the past several years, providing a stable environment for research.

I2P Statistics

The statistics for I2P may be found at http://stats.i2p. The statistics for I2P are more limited than those of Freenet or Tor. The statistics consist of only three categories: exploratory tunnel build, new routers, and router versions. According to I2P, most of the statistics for the platform were gradually removed as the platform matured to improve anonymity.[6]

Brief descriptions of the three available statistics are listed below.

- Exploratory tunnel build: exploratory tunnels are pools of several tunnels, with a tunnel being the connection of multiple routers. So, in other words, it is a very large collection of routers dedicated to a purpose (like a collection of cells working together as a bodily organ). Exploratory tunnels are used by I2P to increase bandwidth and improve connectivity.
- New routers: indicates the number of routers in operation. This measure provides the average over the last twenty-four hours as well as the current number of routers.
- Router version: displays the version of I2P currently being used by routers. Generally, most routers use the current version of I2P, which is beneficial for the security of the platform.

In addition to I2P stats, some individual sites post their statistics publicly. This may be a more useful avenue for research.

Research on the Platforms

A significant amount of original research may be conducted on the platforms themselves. Using the forums on dark web sites, researchers may conduct content analysis of posts to derive themes or user populations.

Recent research in dark web forums explores terrorist activities, freedom from state oppression, victims of domestic violence, and general themes on the platform.[7] Research has been both quantitative (analyzing the number of posts about a certain topic—much more common) and qualitative (analyzing the content of posts). There also has been some effort to interview individuals anonymously via the dark web. The dark web could potentially provide an ultrasecure forum to conduct research interviews.

Some of the most interesting research on the dark web (we believe) is ethnographic studies of the "dark web culture." Ethnography, in a nutshell, means the intensive study of a culture or study group. This research employs qualitative methods to examine the customs of groups, including marginalized cultures like those who use the dark web. It focuses on language as well as practices. This research method is not common in dark web research currently but is emerging.

These forums can also be an excellent place to recruit volunteers for research studies. Remember that among the users of the dark web are many high-risk populations. There are particular procedures for working with these populations, as will likely be stipulated by an organization's institutional review board, or equivalent research ethics panel.

Additionally, it is important in conducting dark web research, particularly in the literature review, to distinguish the term *dark web* as it pertains to anonymous networks (Tor, Freenet, I2P) versus the general term to refer to nefarious online deeds. The distinction between the two uses of the term, as well as the conflation of the term to incorporate the deep web, can result in much irrelevant literature in your search. This distinction was not regularly made until at least 2008.[8]

Each of the three major dark web platforms provides some guidance on needed research. Tor publishes Tech Reports that serve to stimulate research ideas and indicate current concerns. Freenet's documentation section highlights current ideas and trends for the platform. I2P provides a whole section under the "volunteer" tab called "academic research." The introduction to this page opens with the line "I2P is a very unique product that unfortunately has not received the wider academic attention it deserves," so you know they are supportive of research efforts. The site provides a list of known published papers about I2P and highlights areas where new research is needed.

For many individuals and organizations, the role they can serve in dark web research is providing the environment in which the research can be conducted. That means installing dark web platforms on the organization's computers and encouraging intensive research efforts (perhaps by having secure computer labs for projects of this sort).

Reference Interview with Dark Web Resources

Perhaps a more oblique use of the dark web is for Internet searching/reference; however, as a source of knowledge about political dissidents, marginalized victims, crime, and the drug trade, there is a certain value to viewing, and even discussing, real-world cases, rather than simply reading a report. This need not be for scholarly research, but simply for personal knowledge.

Information seekers may also be compelled to peruse dark web wikis, such as the Hidden Wiki (zqktlwi4fecvo6ri.onion). Wikis are collections of information that are collectively organized and supported by the community. Think of Wikipedia, an online dictionary of information that is maintained and updated by anyone on the Internet. Wikis exist as repositories of information on various topics. Important elements of this site are lists of popular dark web site links, a limited timeline of dark web history, and definitions of popular dark web terms and issues. The site covers the entire dark web, but has no illegal content on its own site, giving you a safe peek at the unsavory side of the dark web.

WHAT ABOUT USING SCI-HUB FOR RESEARCH?

While many consider Sci-Hub's repository of free articles a tremendous boon to the academic community, it is important to remember that this website does violate copyright laws in the United States (and many other countries) and has had several lawsuits brought against it. Whether an individual user could be prosecuted for accessing articles from the site is dubious, but is impermissible according to current law. For this reason, we advise not using Sci-Hub in a library setting to access research.

Back-End Research on the Platforms

There has been quite significant research into the back-end design and vulnerabilities of the dark web, dating back to the mid-1990s. Early research attempted to outline the theoretical background upon which an anonymous web platform could be built. The seminal works in this area are Chaum's "The Dining Cryptographer's Problem: Unconditional Sender and Recipient Untraceability"; Reed, Syverson, and Goldschlag's "Proxies for Anonymous Browsing" (seen by some as the underpinning of the entire movement); and Clarke's 1999 thesis, "A Distributed Decentralised

Information Storage and Retrieval System."[9] Clarke's paper, which he wrote as an informatics (information science) student at the University of Edinburgh, is the foundation of Freenet.

The second stage of technical research pertaining to the dark web consisted of fine-tuning the platform. Different approaches were taken to do this, from developing theoretical attacks that could compromise the systems (as discussed in the previous chapter) to designing improvements within the systems. This research, as with the early research, was conducted from a mostly information systems approach. This was necessary with the importance of security and creating a network that does as it claims. The major works of this period include Perry's "Securing the Tor Network" and Cranor et al.'s "FoxTor: A Tor Design Proposal."[10]

The third stage of dark web back-end research is that which is occurring presently. In this stage an emphasis has been placed on making a user-friendly design and expanding the information infrastructure (how we can design the software to be more accessible to the people who will benefit from it). This is an approach more suited to the field of information science, with principles such as metadata management and dark web indexing. Some of these emerging topical works are Jardine's "Privacy, Censorship, Data Breaches and Internet Freedom: The Drivers of Support and Opposition to Dark Web Technologies" and Kundu and Rohatgi's "Generating Queries to Crawl Hidden Web Using Keyword Sampling and Random Forest Classifier."[11]

INFRASTRUCTURE

One of the more important roles an organization can serve is as a participant in the infrastructure initiatives of the dark web. Organizations may do this by providing a safe haven for victims of domestic and sexual violence to receive support, and for individuals to report criminal activities and serve as whistleblowers. Organizations may also host a dark web bridge, through which others' dark web access would be anonymized.

A Safe Haven

Just as libraries long served the role of a safe haven for the acquisition of knowledge from print for those members of at-risk groups, they can serve as a safe haven for responsible dark web use. Marginalized populations that have a legitimate need for the additional privacy the platform provides may also need a secure physical environment in which to access the content. In implementing Tor, consider the populations that may use the platform and what other needs they may have. Consider questions like:

- What other services might these individuals need (e.g., might some users who are victims of violence benefit from having the opportunity to speak with a counselor or social worker)?

- Will users who utilized the dark web for privacy be interested in other privacy options—and will the room configuration (where the computers on which Tor is installed are located) affect these individuals' proclivity to use the platform?
- How can we compromise between users feeling safe to use the dark web and making sure other patrons do not feel uncomfortable about the platforms being made available?

Running a Tor Relay

One of the most helpful roles an individual or organization can serve is as a dark web relay. Serving as a relay strengthens the network and improves speed for all users. This section will specifically discuss the process of establishing a Tor relay; there are ways of establishing relays for Freenet and I2P, though they are very different from Tor (information about which can be found at https://geti2p.net/en/faq and https://freenetproject.org/pages/help.html). The process of setting a Tor relay requires some technical knowledge—but fret not! We are here to guide you.

There are four different types of dark web relays that individuals and organizations may volunteer to run. The first type is the guard relay. The guard relay serves as an entry point for dark web access and thus must handle a large amount of connections. Also, since it is the first connection point, it has the potential to see which IP addresses are connecting to the dark web network (but not with what they are wanting to connect). A guard relay then must be both large and secure.

The second type of relay is known as a middle relay. These relays receive traffic subsequent to the guard relay. Traffic on the dark web is relayed through several of these middle relays to adequately disguise the traffic source.

The traffic eventually reaches an exit relay, which is the final relay in the chain before the traffic connects to the various dark web sites and services. Exit relays are exposed to Internet service providers and web hosts. Any traffic directed through an exit relay displays the relay's IP address. Exit relays handle a high traffic volume and may receive complaints and scrutiny when users access illegal content. While Tor provides guidance and a form letter for exit relays to respond to complaints, this can still be a disconcerting experience for an individual.[12] For this reason, Tor recommends that exit relays be hosted by organizations such as universities and libraries.

Tor runs an FAQ for exit relay operators with legal concerns. Among the questions answered are whether anyone has ever been prosecuted for running a Tor exit relay (no), and how the content of the Digital Millennium Copyright Act pertains to running Tor.

The final relay type is a bridge. While most Tor relays are publicly identifiable, bridges are anonymous, making it harder for Internet service providers to block them. Bridges are particularly needed for users who are accessing the dark web from within oppressive regimes where IP addresses on the dark web relay may be blocked.

As alluded to with the exit relays, all relays have different requirements. All relays, however, require a sizeable bandwidth, often one larger than most home Internet routers can handle. The server on which the relay is maintained should run as frequently as possible to support greater traffic. Guard, middle, and exit relays require the most significant support, with guard and exit necessitating the greatest bandwidth and computer memory. Bridge relays require less bandwidth and can probably be run on an efficient home network.

Most Tor relays are run on Debian, Ubuntu, or BSD. To the nontechnically oriented, these terms may not be familiar—but do not fear, as this guide will show you how to run a relay regardless of your technical knowledge.

RUNNING A SERVER ON A VIRTUAL MACHINE

For those who do not have a Debian/Ubuntu/BSD operating system, there is a method to create one within a Windows or Mac operating system by using a virtual machine. Virtual machines run an operating system on any computer by emulating all the functionality of a dedicated server. Virtual machines can, in fact, be used to host a whole range of services that could not normally be run on a standard personal computer, such as an entire integrated library system. They also can enable Mac users to run Windows applications, and vice versa.

Virtual machines can be downloaded directly from a producer's website, often at no cost. Some of the more common free machines are VirtualBox, VMware, and Windows Virtual PC. Once a virtual machine has been downloaded it will need to be configured to host the type of operating system you need. This can be done on VirtualBox by clicking "New" in the upper-left corner, then selecting an option from the "Type" drop-down menu. To run Ubuntu select "Linux" for the type and "FreeBSD" for the version. For BSD select "BSD" and the type and "FreeBSD" for the version. Name the system and create a virtual hard disk to proceed. To run the operating system, click "Start."

The first step to set up a relay is to add Tor to your operating system of choice. For Debian, enter:

- Printf "deb https://deb.torproject.org/torproject.org jessie main" > /etc/apt/sources.list.d/
- Printf "deb-src https://deb.torproject.org/torproject.org jessie main" > /etc/apt/sources.list.d/
- Gpg—keyserver keys.gnupg.net—recv A3C4F0F979CAA22CDBA8F512EE8CBC9E886DDD89
- Gpg—export A3C4F0F979CAA22CDBA8F512EE8CBC9E886DDD89 / sudo apt-key add –

- $ apt update
- $ apt install tor deb.torproject.org—keyring

For Ubuntu, enter:

- Printf "deb https://deb.torproject.org/torproject.org trusty main" > /etc/apt/sources.list.d/
- Printf "deb-src https://deb.torproject.org/torproject.org trusty main" > /etc/apt/sources.list.d/
- Gpg—keyserver keys.gnupg.net—recv A3C4F0F979CAA22CDBA8F512E E8CBC9E886DDD89
- Gpg—export A3C4F0F979CAA22CDBA8F512EE8CBC9E886DDD89 / sudo apt-key add –
- $ apt update
- $ apt install tor deb.torproject.org—keyring

For BSD, enter within the root shell:

- # pkg install tor
- # cp /usr/local/etc/tor/torrc.sample /usr/local/etc/tor/torrc
- # vim /usr/local/etc/tor/torrc
- 18c18 < SOCKSPort 9050 ---
- > #SOCKSPort 9050 # Default: Bind to localhost:9050 for local connections.
- 38c38 < Log notice file /var/log/tor/notices.log ---
- > #Log notice file /var/log/tor/notices.log
- 42c42 < Log notice syslog ---
- > #Log notice syslog

The second step in the process is to install the relay itself. To install a relay on Debian or Ubuntu:

→ Apt update && apt install tor
→ Nickname (enter a nickname)

ORPort 443
ExitRelay 0
SocksPort 0
ControlSocket 0
ContactInfo (-------@------- enter email)

→ Systemct1 restart tor @ default

To install relay on FreeBSD:

→ Pkg install tor
→ Nickname (enter a nickname)

ORPort 9001
ExitRelay 0

SocksPort 0
ContactInfo (------@------- enter email)
Log notice syslog
   → Sysrc tor_enable = YES
Service tor start
   → Echo "net.inet.ip.random_id=1" >> /etc/sysctl.conf
Sysctl net.inet.ip.random_id=1

Whatever system you use, you should see the following message in your syslog if everything is working properly: "Self-testing indicates your ORPort is reachable from the outside. Excellent. Publishing server descriptor."

The relay will only run so long as the server is running.

ADVOCACY

Perhaps the strongest advocate for the use of the dark web in libraries and organizations is the Library Freedom Project (LFP). The LFP provides several educational tools for libraries pertaining to Internet privacy. It was founded by Alison Macrina, a former librarian at the Watertown (Massachusetts) Free Public Library. In the time since the project's inception, it has successfully helped the Kilton Public Library in Lebanon, New Hampshire, become the first library in the United States to host a Tor relay and successfully defended the library from pressure by the Department of Homeland Security.[13]

The Library Freedom Project provides a list of website links for developing an online privacy class, mobile privacy class, privacy for kids class, privacy for librarians class, and information about Tor at https://libraryfreedomproject.org/resources/. These materials may be used by libraries to promote the adoption of Tor to library employees and patrons. Additionally, the LFP has some other materials that they will provide free of charge to libraries that use Tor, such as informational posters.

The Tor Project website provides less specific materials for advocacy both within organizations and for individuals. On the site's press page is a video about Tor, articles about the dark web, the Tor newsletter, and the Tor blog. The About section of the Tor website may also be used to dispel misconceptions about the platform.

Freenet and I2P both provide some of their own advocacy materials. On Freenet's About page is information about the platform, a video introduction (of nearly two hours' length), as well as downloads of several papers that explore the platform and its benefits. I2P contains tabs on its home page for academic research, guides, and a roadmap. I2P's About page provides a thorough introduction of the platform, comparisons between the major dark web platforms, significant documentation, and tutorials.

A STUDY IN LIBRARY AND ORGANIZATIONAL POLICY

What kinds of changes in library policy might need to be made to accommodate for the use of the dark web? Here are a few sections of policy to consider:

- **What kinds of filtering must we mandate?** As discussed earlier in this book, there are ways to apply a filter on the dark web—though it may compromise privacy. How much filtering is necessary for your institution? Is it better to filter and make the platform available to everyone or not filter and make the platform available only to adults?
- **How do we respond to possible complaints about the service?** Is it acceptable to use the same policy as for challenged books? Who should be responsible for reviewing complaints? Should the technical services administrator be involved?
- **What measures should be taken in response to improper use of the platform?** Do offenders of the policy need to have computer-use privileges revoked?

These portions of policy will need to be considered for any organization that makes computers available to the public. Adhering to a strong policy will limit the capacity of individuals to challenge the policy or organization and likely improve the success of the implementation of the dark web in the organization.

Finally, there are a plethora of periodical articles about the dark web. While many of these are misleading, readers with good information literacy skills (such as librarians) can evaluate these sources for their veracity. The articles can be quite convincing for potential users.

In addition to advocating for dark web use, general advocacy for improved privacy practices can be immensely beneficial to your community. Teaching community members about the dark web can be a small component of a larger lesson that covers such topics as selecting secure passwords, deleting browsing history, and evaluating web sources/pop-ups. The dark web platforms discussed in this book—Tor, Freenet, and I2P—could be discussed alongside some less secure but more mainstream platforms like Firefox and Brave. All these platforms are free and thus lend well to comparison. Let people try them all out and see what they prefer!

FINANCIAL OPPORTUNITY

Many are aware of the Bitcoin trade and the irascible rate of cryptocurrency exchange, but there is also potential for investment in dark web sites. There are no major legitimate marketplaces like eBay, Walmart, or Amazon on the dark web. There are many products that are legal to purchase, but may be embarrassing to purchase (e.g., contraceptive devices), and this may make a legitimate marketplace on the dark web a successful endeavor.

As the dark web becomes more widely accepted, there may be employment opportunities for web developers. Industries looking for programmers will want those who are experienced with the platform. The dark web platforms themselves often seek developers.

Another opportunity as the dark web grows is to identify a marketing strategy for the platform. The dark web eliminates the direct marketing strategies used by companies, wherein they use your browsing history to market products based on those you have previously viewed. While this practice is typically considered an unwanted invasion of privacy, it is a multibillion dollar industry for the companies that employ the technique. Strategies to compromise the privacy of the dark web with this booming Internet marketing industry could be extremely profitable.

The Internet in itself represents a gross domestic product of nearly $1 trillion (US), which equals almost 2 percent of the gross world product (the economic output of the entire world).[14] The dark web represents an untapped area for budding (hopefully legitimate) entrepreneurs.

CONCLUSION

The dark web can be intimidating. The stories that are told of illegal affairs and immoral actions are enough to make most users feel the platform is not right for them. But this belief is mistaken. The dark web brings a lot of good and has the potential to improve the privacy and security of the world population and perhaps even bolster democracy on the global stage. There are so many ways for the dark web to be used and so many ways for you, the reader, to become involved. Join us in preserving, defending, and promoting the dark web. Help us cast light on the platform for others and serve your part in dispelling persistent myths about it.

NOTES

1. Everett M. Rogers, *Diffusion of Innovations*, 5th ed. (New York, NY: Free Press, 2003).

2. American Library Association Council, "Core Values of Librarianship," June 29, 2004, http://www.ala.org/advocacy/intfreedom/corevalues.

3. Roger C. Greer, Robert J. Grover, and Susan G. Fowler, *Introduction to the Library and Information Professions*, 2nd ed (Santa Barbara, CA: Libraries Unlimited, 2013).

4. The Tor Project, "About Tor Metrics," accessed May 5, 2018, https://metrics.torproject.org/about.html.

5. Oxford Internet Institute, "The Anonymous Internet," June 9, 2014, https://geography.oii.ox.ac.uk/the-anonymous-Internet/.

6. I2P Project, "I2P Stats," accessed March 25, 2019, stats.i2p.

7. Tianjun Fu, Ahmed Abbasi, and Hsinchun Chen, "A Focused Crawler for Dark Web Forums," *Journal of the Association for Information Science and Technology* 61, no. 6 (2010): 1213–231; Yulei Zhang, Shuo Zeng, Li Fan, Yan Dang, Catherine A. Larson, and Hsinchun Chen, "Dark Web Forums Portal: Searching and Analyzing Jihadist Forums," Proceedings of the 2009 IEEE International Conference on Intelligence and Security Informatics (Dallas, TX, June 2009), 71–76; Robert W. Gehl, "Power/Freedom on the Dark Web: A Digital Ethnography of the Dark Web Social Network," *New Media and Society* 18, no. 7 (2014): 1219–235.

8. Damon McCoy, Kevin Bauer, Dirk Grunwald, Tadayoshi Kohno, and Douglas Sicker, "Shining Light in Dark Places: Understanding the Tor Network," Proceedings of the 8th International Symposium on Privacy Enhancing Technologies (Leuven, Belgium, July 2008), 63–76.

9. David Chaum, "The Dining Cryptographer's Problem: Unconditional Sender and Recipient Untraceability," *Journal of Cryptology* 1, no. 1 (1988): 65–75; Michael G. Reed, Paul F. Syverson, and David M. Goldschlag, "Proxies for Anonymous Routing," Proceedings of the 12th Annual Computer Security Applications Conference (San Diego, CA, December 1996); Ian Clarke, "A Distributed Decentralised Information Storage and Retrieval System" (master's thesis, University of Edinburgh, 1999), http://citeseerx.ist.psu.edu/viewdoc/download?doi=10.1.1.32.3665&rep=rep1&type=pdf.

10. Mike Perry, "Securing the Tor Network," 2007, https://www.blackhat.com/presentations/bh-usa-07/Perry/Whitepaper/bh-usa-07-perry-WP.pdf; Lorrie F. Cranor, Serge Egelman, Jason Hong, Ponnurangam Kumaraguru, Cynthia Kuo, Sasha Romanosky, Janice Tsai, and Kami Vaniea, "FoxTor: A Tor Design Proposal," November 30, 2005, http://cups.cs.cmu.edu/pubs/TorGUIContest113005.pdf.

11. Eric Jardine, "Privacy, Censorship, Data Breaches and Internet Freedom: The Drivers of Support and Opposition to Dark Web Technologies," *New Media and Society* 20, no. 8 (2017): 2824–843; Sabarni Kundu and Shwetanshu Rohatgi, "Generating Queries to Crawl Hidden Web Using Keyword Sampling and Random Forest Classifier," *International Journal of Advanced Research in Computer Science* 8, no. 9 (2017): 337–41.

12. The Tor Project, "The Tor Relay Guide," accessed May 4, 2018, https://trac.torproject.org/projects/tor/wiki/TorRelayGuide.

13. Library Freedom Project, "Tor Exit Relays in Libraries: A New LFP Project," July 28, 2015, https://libraryfreedomproject.org/torexitpilotphase1, and "Libraries, Tor, Freedom, and Resistance," September 11, 2015, https://libraryfreedomproject.org/libraries-tor-freedom-and-resistance/.

14. Stephen E Siwek, "Measuring the US Internet Sector," December 10, 2015, https://cdn1.Internetassociation.org/wp-content/uploads/2015/12/Internet-Association-Measuring-the-US-Internet-Sector-12-10-15.pdf.

9

Reaping the Rewards of the Dark Web

A TALE OF THE INTERNET PAST

In 1996, Debora Spar and Jeffrey Bussgang published an article in the *Harvard Business Review* entitled "Ruling the Net." Note that the Internet was not available for public use until 1990, and only about 11 percent of the United States population had access to the Internet in 1996.[1] This was a year before Google and four years before Wikipedia, and Amazon was merely an online bookseller struggling to make a profit. The Internet was an amorphous spattering of what it is today. It was, in many regards, a Wild West. Few people used it, many had little conception of what it was, and there was little to suggest how powerful and useful it would become to just about every person in the developing and developed world. In fact, many major organizations, such as the Smithsonian, Walmart, and virtually the entire music recording industry, initially refused to promote their products online, for fear that there would be little retribution against those who infringed on copyright. However, as Spar and Bussgang noted,

> In surveying this frontier, it is important to realize that the current lack of rules does not necessarily mean that governments will send in the cavalry or that companies will walk away in despair, leaving the Internet to the hackers and the chat lines. Instead, it

simply means that companies need to think carefully before making any headlong leaps into cyberspace.[2]

Spar and Bussgang recognized the potential in the Internet to connect people, provide comfort, and increase business, and argued that the absence of the realization of this growth came from a lack of rules. They suggested that, even if governments could not enforce laws, there were ways to create communities online that could enforce rules. The authors argued, "What they [companies and users] need, in short, is an entity to transform the anonymity and anarchy of the Internet into a market with identifiable customers and recordable transactions."[3] Note, again, that this article is discussing the Internet—the World Wide Web—circa 1996. But it sounds very similar to the arguments made about the dark web throughout this book, doesn't it? What changed, and what impact can this have on your dark web experience?

Simply enough, investment.

Investment in monetary capital but also time investment by programmers who developed secure infrastructures and, most important, adoption of the Internet by companies and users alike. Organizations saw value to using the Internet for internal communications, using technologies like email, and developing information systems capable of distributing information across the web to geographically disparate areas. The more users who adopted the Internet, the more interested legitimate companies became in creating services on the web. The promise of a gold rush on the Internet— with low overhead costs and the ability to sell products across the entire globe—led to a massive boom in dot-com websites in the late 1990s. This, ultimately, led to the dot-com crash in the early 2000s, from which the surviving sites were strengthened into globally recognizable brands.

By the mid-2000s, there was no question that the Wild West had been tamed. The number of legitimate users of the Internet far outnumbered the wrongdoers and the attention brought to the Internet heightened the imperative among law enforcement agencies to crack down on cybercriminals. Certainly, there was (and still is) cybercrime on the Internet, but it no longer intimidates organizations or users from using the service. The Internet has become a crucial component of our world. For some people, it is essentially an additional organ (admittedly, the authors of this publication included).

So what does the dark web need in order to become legitimized like the Internet? We would contend that the answer is "You!" So, if we haven't convinced you yet to go explore the dark web for yourself (or even create your own site!), let us have one more crack at it. Consider this our elevator speech of what benefits the dark web provides for you.

THE BIG PITCH

First, we want to reiterate that it is *not* illegal to use the dark web within the United States. It is illegal (of course) to intentionally access illegal content *anywhere* on the

Internet, but there is *a lot* of content on the dark web that is perfectly legal (just like the regular Internet with which you are familiar).

Second, the dark web is not run by some malevolent Darth Vader–type overlord. It is just a network. It does not care what you do on it—it just "is." It's like a baseball. Could you do damage with it? Yes. You could also play baseball with it. And the ball—it doesn't care either way.

So, what does the dark web hold for you?

Privacy and security the likes of which the regular Internet could never afford. While it is not impossible for law enforcement to track down a criminal on the dark web, it takes an extraordinary effort that is reserved for those who are that: criminals. For those who are conducting normal business and want enhanced privacy, there is only the most remote chance that your privacy could ever be breached on the dark web. Conversely, on the regular Internet it would simply take someone with a good knowledge of computers and the web, a little time, and a mild vendetta against you to completely wreck your entire Internet existence.

Freedom from unwanted tracking and targeted advertising. If advertisers are able to collect data about what you are viewing on Amazon and send you ads on other web pages, then what other information could they have and what could they do with it? The answer is that it depends on the sites you are using.

Facebook's privacy policy (as of this writing, last revised in April 2018) is approximately 4,250 words, slightly less than double the length of this chapter. If you include the terms of use (which are referenced frequently in the privacy policy), then you are at about 8,000 words. If you read, and understand, all of that, what you will find is that Facebook has broad powers to use your data and share it with "partners" located "in the United States or other countries outside of where you live for the purposes as described in this policy."[4] The partners, per the policy, include advertisers, measurement partners, partners offering goods and services in Facebook products, vendors and service partners, researchers, and law enforcement. Examples of data that you give them permission to collect include:

- "The content, communications and other information you provide . . . including when you sign up for an account, create or share content, and message or communicate with others." This includes metadata about the content, "such as the location of a photo or the date a file was created."[5]
- "Your usage": when and how you use Facebook products.[6]
- "Information about transactions made on our Products," including "payment information, such as your credit or debit card number and other card information; other account and authentication information; and billing, shipping and contact details."[7]
- "Things others do and information they provide about you": Anything in others' posts about you is included.[8]

Of course, Facebook is certainly not the only site that collects this type of data. This is standard for most sites. Facebook, for its part, does its data collection overtly by having you create an account and agree to the terms. Other sites may collect data in the background while you are navigating, which you may not even realize you have given them permission to do.

The same general functionality as your current browsing experience. As discussed throughout this book, the Tor browser looks very similar to a traditional Internet browser (because it is just a modified Firefox browser). Navigating the browser will not prove difficult for those who have used Firefox (and even those who have not). The only difficulty is the site addresses. Fortunately, chapter 6 is chock-full of sites just waiting for you to visit. In other words, "It's too hard to learn" is not a legitimate excuse.

The chance to get in on the ground level of something big. Opportunities for businesses and individuals are aplenty. The most important thing in business and in life is the right timing. That time is now! The early hurdles of the dark web have been overcome, just as occurred with the early Internet. Are we on the precipice of the dark web boom? If the adoption of other anonymous technologies like Bitcoin are any indication, the answer may very well be yes!

So download a dark web browser now and give it a chance for yourself.

FINAL WORDS

Let us debrief.

In this book, we have discussed the dark web, from what it is, to how it works, to what you can do with it and why you should care. We have tried to provide a thorough guide that avoids sensationalism and gives you the straight facts that you deserve. Undoubtedly, we have not touched on every question you might have about the dark web, but hope we have answered enough to encourage you to research further.

Now we would like to take a moment to talk about how we believe you can get the most out of the dark web as a user. It is important to us that we not only encourage people to use the dark web, but to use it appropriately, in a way that will support its growth and legitimacy. So here are a few tips:

- There is a certain intrigue that draws people to gather in groups and "explore" the dark web as if it is some mystic cave and you might expect a three-headed dragon to appear. This has likely only grown in frequency with recent television and movie productions that make browsing the dark web like something out of a slasher film. First of all, we think that if you give the dark web a legitimate chance, you will realize that it is absolutely nothing like those portrayals. Second, please don't. Often in society, believing is believing, meaning that a kernel of truth (for instance, that there are some sites on the dark web that have illegal content) can easily be popped into a giant piece of popcorn that suffocates reality. Playing games where you look up illegal dark web sites—other than the fact that it is still illegal, no matter how and where you access them—can create misperceptions that subconsciously crystalize and make you believe that the dark web is only illegal content and has no redeeming value. That is, of course, detrimental to the dark web networks, but it also deprives you of the opportunity to experience what the dark web is really about.

- Think not what the dark web can do for you . . . think about what you can do with the dark web. How could you use the secure messaging platforms on the dark web? What about writing an entire crowdsourced novel by anonymous authors, or sharing your thoughts with an anonymous sympathetic crowd? Do not limit yourself to what the dark web is currently. Think about what new opportunities the technology could provide for you.
- See the dark web for its role in society, rather than the role in which it can serve you. Some readers of this book may find little personal value to the dark web. Perhaps you do not use the Internet much, or you just do not care about privacy. Maybe none of the sites of the dark web interest you, and you do not have the interest or knowledge to create your own. If that is the case, we ask that you look at the dark web through the eyes of someone who would use it. Do not neglect it. It is important to have supporters from all walks of life. If you see value in the dark web for others, then be an active advocator!

THE END

Our objective in writing this book is to dispel myths and espouse benefits of the dark web. We hope, at the very least, that you now have a better understanding (even appreciation) for the dark web and the important role it can serve for certain populations. As library and information professionals, we hope that our book ignites a passion in some readers to research further, explore the dark web yourself, and think about new beneficial ways in which the dark web can be used. Currently, much of the discussion about the dark web, even among academics, lacks any scholarly integrity. There is an almost hedonistic delight, it seems, among some media outlets and individuals to paint the dark web as evil and look no further. In the future, we hope these discussions will include the merits, and demerits, of the networks themselves, rather than a whole lot of misinformation and dismissal.

The Internet and dark web are advocacy-driven platforms. This book, insofar as it can be, is an education and advocacy tool. We sincerely hope that it does not merely become a quick read that you discard, but that you will apply and expand upon what we have shared and spread these ideas. If you think the dark web is something worth preserving, then do something about it. Let's get to work!

NOTES

1. International Telecommunications Union, "Internet Users per 100 Inhabitants 1997 to 2007," accessed August 3, 2018, http://www.itu.int/ITU-D/ict/statistics/ict.

2. Debora Spar and Jeffrey Bussgang, "Ruling the Net," *Harvard Business Review* 74, no. 3 (May-June 1996): 126.

3. Ibid, 127.

4. Facebook, Inc., "Data Policy," April 19, 2018, https://www.facebook.com/policy.php.

5. Ibid.

6. Ibid.

7. Ibid.

8. Ibid.

Index

About the Authors

Matthew Beckstrom was born and raised in Montana. He received an associate's degree in computer science from the University of Montana and then a bachelor's degree in computer science from Montana State University. After working in various technology jobs, he finally settled into the job of systems manager at the Lewis & Clark Library in Helena in 1999. In 2012, he received his master's degree in information science from the University of North Texas after receiving a grant from the Montana State Library to attend library school.

Matthew has had a long interest in privacy, security, and intellectual freedom. He has been teaching and presenting for almost twenty years on a variety of library, technology, and privacy topics. He started teaching at Helena College in 2013. He has taught various classes including computer programming, Linux, and computer modeling.

Matthew is active at the local and national level, serving on various boards and committees. He is currently a member of the Montana Library Association Board and serves on the government affairs committee and the intellectual freedom committee for the association. He is also a board member for the ACLU of Montana. Nationally, he is on the American Library Association Council, serves on the conference committee, and is the liaison to the intellectual freedom committee from the Library and Information Technology Association Board.

Matthew has written several books and guides on privacy and intellectual freedom, as well as various articles and blog posts on technology.

You can find more about Matthew on his website: www.matthewbeckstrom.com.

Brady Lund is a PhD student at Emporia State University's School of Library and Information Management. He holds a master's of library science from Emporia State and a bachelor's in communication science and disorders from Wichita State

University. He has published articles in several major library and information science journals on topics ranging from information security to knowledge organization, and he initially presented on the topic of the dark web at the 2017 American Library Association Annual Conference.

Lightning Source UK Ltd.
Milton Keynes UK
UKHW041252260421
382646UK00001B/1